Living with Flowers

LAURENCE KING

Published in 2019 by
Laurence King Publishing Ltd
361–373 City Road
London
EC1V 1LR
United Kingdom
T + 44 (0)20 7841 6900
F + 44 (0)20 7841 6910
enquiries@laurenceking.com
www.laurenceking.com

A catalogue record for this book is
available from the British Library.

ISBN: 978-1-78627-399-4

Printed in China

Photography: James Stopforth
Design: Masumi Briozzo

Rowan Blossom

Living with Flowers

**Blooms & Bouquets
for the Home**

Laurence King Publishing

Contents

Rowan Blossom's World	**6**
Toolkit	12
Floral Foam	16
Vessels	17
Conditioning	18
Chapter I: Everyday	**23**
Bottles, Jam Jars & Bud Vases	26
Dinky Posy in a Vase	30
Kitchen Blooms in a Jug	34
Dried Flower Arrangement	38
In a Pickle	40
Candlestick with a Floral Touch	46
Floral Wreath	50
Chapter II: Entertaining	**55**
Floral Place Settings	58
Flowery Cake Stand	62
Floral Garnishes	66
Table Garland	68
Compote Arrangement	74
Showstopper Urn	80

Chapter III: Giving	**85**
Choosing Flowers for Bouquets	88
Bouquet	92
Little Vase Arrangement	96
Pressed Flowers	100
Blooms for Houseguests	102
Bowl of Blooms	104
Chapter IV: Fashion	**109**
Corsage	112
Big, Blowsy & Bold Flower Crown	116
Botanical Makeup	120
Chapter V: Party	**125**
Blooming Chandelier	128
Flower Curtain	134
Meadow Box	138
Bloom Bonbon	144
Archway	150
Blossomary	**161**
Practical Stuff	162
Seasonal Heroes	166
Index	172
Thanks	174

Rowan Blossom's World

> **'I hope this book will convey the excitement I've found working with flowers, and give you the confidence to have a go yourself.'**

Blossom symbolizes vitality and the reason why I believe flowers should be embraced in our lives and homes. When I spot the first signs of blossom, my heart skips a beat, as there is the ice-melting reassurance that winter is finally over and spring has arrived. It gives hope that the days will be getting longer and lighter.

After this initial sighting, clouds of blossom seem to erupt everywhere, to the point where you cannot escape it. Plumes of petals cluster on burdened branches, the colour spectrum ranging from snow white to ballet slipper blush, on to candyfloss pink and finishing with a crescendo of cerise pops. The streets are transformed from mundane to magical, and it feels as though you're walking on a movie set – which I guess I sort of am, being a Notting Hill girl! The spectacle is overwhelmingly joyful.

Soon enough the swells of blossom start to drop and they flutter and dance in the air, and suddenly, almost overnight, the blossoms shatter and litter the streets with a bucolic confetti. The fleeting nature of the blossom season is a reminder to appreciate the here and now. For me, these are the key reasons why flowers are so important in our everyday lives: they bring hope, give you joy and force you to live in the moment.

I came to flowers during my mid-twenties, while working in the fashion industry. I realized my change of allegiance when one of the most joyful, if not the most joyful thing, about going to Paris during Fashion Week was to visit my favourite florists in the Marais! I would become over-excited and coo over how much more gorgeous flowers were in Paris and greedily buy big bundles of blooms, without even considering the logistics of getting them back to London on the Eurostar – which was always full of jaded but fabulous fashionistas on their final leg home after the gruelling month away for the shows.

Wanting to get a better understanding of the technical aspects of floristry, I enrolled in a part-time, six-month course in London. It was the perfect solution for me as I was able to keep my job in fashion while learning the basics and plotting how to start my business. It also made me realize what an affinity there is between fashion and flowers, as both are intrinsically informed by colour, pattern, line and form.

After finishing the course I opened a little pop-up florist in a vintage furniture shop in Notting Hill. A fearless naivety made me think this was the thing to do to get Rowan Blossom on the map, and in a way it did. Having had absolutely no experience working in a florist before, this certainly made me learn on my feet very quickly! The pop-up was a short-lived but sweet three months, after which I gratefully hung up my apron and vowed that a flower shop was not for me. Being a one-woman team meant I was up at 3am every day doing the buying at the flower market, conditioning the blooms and foliage myself, organizing the styling and visual merchandising, working on the shop floor and delivering everything by hand. I was also having to deal with all the trappings of being a business owner: admin, emails, accounts, all those important but extremely dull tasks! With hindsight, it was bonkers even to consider it, but it gave me the kick-start I needed and reassurance that I had made the right decision in taking the leap. I was totally, utterly spellbound by the blooms, and knew that all I wanted was to work with flowers.

Since then I have been studio-based at a little place on the fringe of Notting Hill, and the business has flourished. I predominantly work on fashion events, parties and weddings, but what I love more than anything is creating flower arrangements for people's homes.

I love what I do, and always try to do it with enthusiasm and a smile, no matter how early I arrive at the flower market! I am so very lucky to be pursuing a career that I dreamed of. The dream at times has been demanding (and on occasion nightmarish!), but flowers are joyous, and you cannot help but be uplifted by them.

When I started writing this book I wanted to create something that was inspiring but that also offered practical advice; the sort of book I would have pored over when I was first exploring the idea of going into flowers as a career. I have a small library of floristry books, all of which are well thumbed and loved, dog-eared and watermarked from my various attempts at home floristry before starting the business. While this is by no means a reference book on everything you need to know about floristry, I hope it will convey the excitement I have found working with flowers. I wanted to share with you some of the hints and tips I've gained on this journey, to give you the confidence to have a go yourself.

Toolkit

My toolkit is something of a magician's hat masquerading as a tradesman's toolbox, and you will come across all sorts of bizarre implements. Some are not the least bit glamorous or items you would immediately associate with floristry.

During the last rummage I came across not one but three different saws, an industrial staple gun and a power drill, contrasting with the fripperies of hand-dyed silk ribbon, pearl-headed pins and calligraphy pens. Odd! Bits and pieces that are mentioned throughout the book, and which would be worth having in your armoury, include:

Baby bottle sterilizing tablets – keep water looking fresh and sparkly. Don't overdo it; I usually crumble a little bit into bud vases, bottles and jars, a quarter of a tablet into small or medium vases, and a whole tablet into big pickle jars.

Bind wire – be warned, this is slightly oiled, and using it covers your hands in black slicks that require a lot of scrubbing to remove (Swarfega hand cleaner is genius). It is used because it is robust and incredibly strong. As an alternative you can use plastic-coated gardening wire.

Cable ties – probably the one thing I rely on most in my toolkit. I don't know where I would be without these wonders, as I use them for pretty much every event I do. I have them in every size and length imaginable. I always go for black, as it is easier to cover than white.

Cellophane – I always use transparent cellophane, the thickest I can find. The cheaper stuff can split easily, which is far from ideal when you are relying on it to keep a bouquet hydrated, or to stop a leaky vessel from spilling water everywhere.

Chicken wire – you wouldn't believe how many rolls of this I go through in the studio. It is a florist's secret weapon, especially when avoiding floral foam. It is malleable enough to be squashed into containers and provides enough support to dainty stems to keep flowers where you want them.

Coated wire/twine/string – any of these are useful when it comes to tying bouquets.

Dustpan and brush – because nobody wants an untidy work station.

Floral foam (Oasis) – more on this on page 16.

Florist adhesive tack – this comes on a big roll, like a thick sausage of liquorice. You work pieces in your hands and the warmth transforms the tack into a sticky, gummy consistency. It's waterproof, too.

Florist aluminium wire – I discovered this about a year into my floristry career and it changed everything for me when it comes to making flower crowns, as it is easy to shape but sturdy enough to hold the weight of flowers. It is available in a rainbow of metallic colours, which for the magpie in me is an absolute dream.

Florist pot tape – brilliant waterproof tape that you can tear with your hands (no snips needed). It is essential for keeping chicken wire in place.

Florist scissors – this is the one piece of kit that you will need for every single recipe in this book, and in fact whenever you are working with flowers. I use Sakagen scissors, which are made in Japan, and despite looking unassuming they are samurai-sword sharp. You have been warned, so please approach with caution! Although they are a little more costly than your usual scissors, think of them as an investment both in time (you can whip through conditioning so much quicker with them) and also in your poor hands, as they are ergonomically designed to use minimal strength for maximal slice.

Florist tape – either Stemtex, which is a papery, gummed tape, or Parafilm tape, which is plastic-based. Both are self sealing and waterproof, so when the end of a flower stem is wrapped in it the moisture is locked in – perfect for situations when the flower will be out of water, such as on a flower crown or in a buttonhole/corsage, to keep things looking perky.

Foliage stripper – these flexible plastic discs are covered in nodules

My trusty Sakagen florist scissors.

and can speed up conditioning. The nodules grip the foliage and pull it off.

Gardening gloves – invest in a good pair that is nimble enough for you to have a good grip on the task at hand, but that will also protect your skin. These are particularly useful when handling spiky chicken wire. (If only I had invested in a pair of these beauties sooner I would have avoided many trips to the first-aid kit!)

Hand cream – essential after a long day working with your hands. I particularly love Aesop Resurrection Aromatique, because it does feel as though it gives your hands new life, and for the heavenly scent and pink packaging.

Heavy-duty secateurs or loppers – for anything the Japanese scissors can't cut through, such as woody foliage stems.

Knife – this can be a simple kitchen table knife or a specialist florist one. It doesn't really matter, as we only use it to slice up soaked blocks of floral foam.

Lazy Susan – one of my most used and loved companions in the studio, she is anything but lazy! A genius invention by the French, who called them *étagères*, these rotating serving trays have come to be loved by florists far and wide. When assembling an arrangement, place it on your lazy Susan and rotate so you can see it from different angles.

Metal pin holder or 'frog' – place these at the bottom of your vessel and spear stems directly on to them. Secure with florist adhesive tack to prevent any wobbles.

Nylon fishing wire – let's be clear (no pun intended), this transparent wire has many uses and can help you to create floral illusions.

Pins – you can keep it simple with a flat-headed seamstress pin or go for something pretty like a pearl head. Use to attach buttonholes and corsages.

Plastic dust sheets – I have a few huge tarpaulins that are used to cover boats in winter. These can be laid down in marquees for big installations, and I always keep a stash of disposable decorating ones for anything on a smaller scale. They can also be used to line mantelpieces/stairwells/banisters

if you want to make sure you don't cause any damage.

Plastic florist test tubes – nifty little vessels that will remind you of chemistry lessons at school, only they are plastic instead of glass and come with a tiny rubber cap. I love these as they are reusable. Fill them with water, pop the rubber cap on and poke the stem into the water. They are brilliant in garlands; you can tape them on to long sticks to add height to large arrangements, or use them in foam-free constructions.

Ribbon – my ribbon box brings me a ridiculous amount of joy. I could eulogize about grosgrain and bore you for hours about different luxuries of velvet, and don't get me started on natural hand-dyed silks.

Sharp snips or wire cutters – to get through chicken wire.

Spray bottle – you can pick them up cheaply at your local garden centre, and they are the best thing to revive your arrangements. I have, as usual, gone full throttle on this and have an industrial-sized pressure sprayer that holds 8 litres and comes with a shoulder strap, so you can casually stroll around with it attached to you at all times. So chic.

Sticky-backed (Command) hooks – if you want to create an installation that hangs from the ceiling or is attached to the wall, but can't or don't want to drill holes or bang in nails, these are your solution! They take seconds to install, don't leave a mark, and can be reused – they deserve a round of applause.

Stub wire – available in lots of different gauges and lengths. The lower the gauge number, the thicker the wire (confusing, I know). I tend to have a very fine one (32) for delicate wiring, a medium one that covers most flowers (24) and a heavy-duty one (18 or 20) for very thick stems.

Watering can – to top up your vases and vessels without disrupting the arrangement.

Extra items that you may need for the recipes in this book, but that aren't used repeatedly, include cake stands, carabiner clips, card or paper, hanging-basket cages, ice-cube trays, adhesive tape, strong rope or chain, and a wire wreath ring base.

Floral Foam

The debate about floral foam (often referred to as the brand name Oasis) in floristry is as divisive as the British squabble about Marmite: you either love it or hate it. Some florists love it for its ease of use, structural stability and mass-marketed availability. Many more loathe it because it is not biodegradable and it contains all sorts of nasty chemicals that are harmful to humans and the environment alike.

So, most florists have chosen to turn their back on it. My personal stance is that whenever possible I go foam-free, preferring to use chicken wire, moss and other contraptions to keep flowers where they should be. But I would be dishonest if I claimed not to use it in some designs, when time is against me or the logistics seem nigh on impossible.

I have used floral foam in some of these recipes because I want them to be simple and accessible, but where there is an alternative I have outlined this in the text.

Floral foam has a slightly mercurial quality: when dry it is dusty and chalky to the touch, but when soaked it transforms into a soft, fudgy consistency.

To soak it properly, fill a sink or large bucket with cold water. Floral foam absorbs water like a sponge. Place it on top of the water and it will slowly sink just below the surface.

Be mindful about the depth of water, as the level will drop as absorption takes place. Don't be tempted to push the block into the water or pour water over it, as this will cause air pockets to form inside. If this happens the flower stems will not get the moisture they need.

When it is fully soaked, the foam will have transformed from sage green to dark evergreen, and will bob up and down near the surface of the water. It takes about 5 minutes for an average-sized block to be fully soaked.

Leave it on the kitchen draining board for about an hour to dry out a little. You can use soaked foam straight away if it is destined for a tray or other watertight vessel, but bear in mind that as you stick stems into it water will squirt out.

For floral foam that is going into a hanging installation, such as the Blooming Chandelier (see p. 128) or the Bloom Bonbon (see p. 144), I would soak it the day before and let it dry out overnight to avoid any drips.

When inserting stems into foam, make sure you cut the stem at a sharp angle so that you can spear the foam easily.

Here I am using pre-soaked floral foam cut in shape to provide the basis for a Floral Candlestick (see p. 46).

Vessels

Over the years I've collected lots of vessels, and my studio shelves groan under the ever-growing hoard: old miniature poison bottles, Granny's finest cut crystal, antique silver rose bowls and tankards, painted ceramic water jugs, bronze egg cups, vintage pickle and Chinese ginger jars, and a mass of compotes, bowls, urns and glassware in all manner of shapes, heights and sizes.

When it comes to vessels the only requisite is that it is, or can be made, watertight, since without water your flowers won't survive for very long. Sometimes the vessel is as important aesthetically as the arrangement itself, as with the Kitchen Blooms in a Jug (see p. 34), and other times the mechanics will be discreetly hidden so the blooms are the stars of the show, as with the Meadow Box (see p. 138).

At home I like to keep a small selection of vessels that are tried and tested, and these feature in this book – bud vases, bottles and jars, ceramic jugs, footed bowls and a variety of vases from small to large in ceramic and glass. Most of these things are readily available online, but I also advocate rummaging in car-boot sales, auction houses and vintage markets for one-off finds that you can fall in love with.

A selection of my large collection of bud vases, jam jars and bottles for making small posies (see p. 26).

Conditioning

Conditioning is the backbone of successful floristry and happy, healthy blooms. A quick glance at the *Oxford English Dictionary* reveals that to condition is to 'bring (something) into the desired state for use'. When applied to flowers and foliage, proper preparation will ensure that they look their best, and that they live as long as possible. Essentially, it means you will get the best value out of your blooms as they will look beautiful and last longer.

The process can be a little fiddly and time-consuming, but it is therapeutic in the sense that once you have the technique figured out you can lose yourself in the task at hand. Consider wearing gloves if your skin is particularly sensitive, although they can inhibit your dexterity. Make sure you always wear them when handling euphorbia, as this plant produces a milky sap that can irritate the skin. Similar care is needed with monkshood and foxgloves, both of which are poisonous by ingestion.

Ideally, conditioning should be done the moment you get the flowers into your house. If this isn't possible, the very least you should do is get them into water and, if time permits, give the stems a bit of a snip to encourage the flowers to take up fresh water.

How to condition:
1. Fill as many buckets as you require with cold, clean water mixed with flower food. Make sure the buckets are clean: dirty buckets will sully the water and cause the flowers to become sad and droopy, which is not what we want!

2. Flower food often comes attached to the flower wrap, but if not I tend to chuck a little sugar into the water to give a little pep, or add a baby bottle sterilizing tablet. Some florists suggest using bleach and vinegar to keep the water clear, but I avoid this and generally just make sure to change the water when necessary.

3. Remove any foliage, leaves, tendrils or thorns from the lower two-thirds of each stem. Any foliage that is left on the stem below the water line of your vase will rot and cause bacteria to form, which will make your flowers miserable.

4. Check the quality of the flower head and if necessary 'petal pick'. This is normally reserved for roses, whose petals can easily becomed damaged and brown. The best thing to do is firmly pinch any offending petals at the base to remove them from the flower head.

5. Trim the bottom of all stems with sharp scissors or secateurs. You want to avoid jagged edges, as they can encourage decay, so the sharper your snips the better. Cut at an angle to encourage the stem to take up as much water

as possible; a horizontal cut will mean the stem sits flush with the bottom of the bucket, inhibiting drinking ability.

6. Place the conditioned stems in a bucket of cold, clean water (generally you want it to be deep enough to submerge half of the stem) and leave somewhere cool for at least a couple of hours before you start to work with them. If you have the time to do this the day before and leave overnight, even better, as the more water they can take on before you handle them, the happier and healthier the flowers will be.

7. Once the flowers have had their time in the bucket and you are ready to arrange them, recut the stems to the required length for your arrangement.

Tips flower by flower:
Certain flowers require different types of attention when it comes to conditioning, so I've outlined some tips below:

Amaryllis – the stems tend to curl up when left in water, so to prevent this bind the base of the stem with a tight wrap of adhesive tape.

Anemone – one of the simplest flowers to condition, as they have a silky-smooth stem, although sometimes I remove the foliage frill around the head if it looks tired. They have a slightly capricious nature and keep growing once they are cut, so bear this in mind when including them in your arrangements.

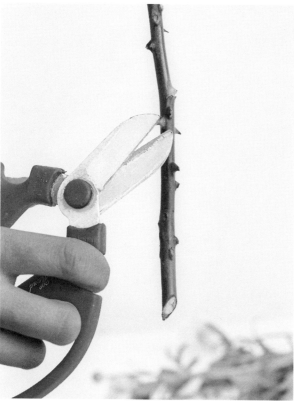

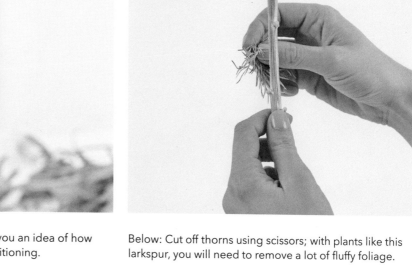

Top: Before-and-after pictures give you an idea of how many leaves to remove during conditioning.

Below: Cut off thorns using scissors; with plants like this larkspur, you will need to remove a lot of fluffy foliage.

Astrantia – can be incredibly fickle, and will either be your shining star and stand upright for days, or collapse into a flop. If it flops I bind it tightly in tissue paper, recut the stems then stand them in cool water with lots of flower food, which usually revives it.

Daffodil – I always remove the papery husks, just because I think it looks prettier (time-consuming but worth it!). When cut, the stems exude a sap that can kill other flowers if left in the same bucket, so keep them separate until you start arranging.

Delphinium, amaryllis and lupin – all have hollow stems, the perfect in-built water receptacle! Turn the flower upside down over a bucket, fill the stem with water and plug the end closed with cotton wool to keep these blooms super-fresh.

Delphinium and larkspur – remove all the spindly little tendrils that grow up the stem, but don't throw these chaps away: they can be used in arrangements to give a wilder, more natural feel.

Foxglove – tends to grow towards the light, so the stems can become quite wiggly. I personally don't mind this, as I love the way they dance towards the sun, but if you want to keep a uniform appearance, turn the bucket every day or so.

Hydrangea – need lots of water (hence the name, which derives from the Greek *hydro*, meaning 'water'). If the flower starts to look sad and wilted, submerge the whole head in a bucket of cold water; it may look strange but the flower can drink through its petals, so this is the best way to revive them.

Lilac – another flighty flower that can suddenly droop. A snip up the stem and lots of flower food will give it the best chance.

Peony – to encourage them to open, either submerge the bud in warm water or hold it under a running tap. The water will dissolve the sticky sugary coating that cloaks the bud, and give it a gentle nudge towards opening.

Poppy and hellebore – can be prone to drooping, so benefit from having their stems sealed. I do this by wrapping the top third of the stem tightly in tissue paper and plunging the bottom of the stem into just-boiled water. Leave in the water until cooled and unwrap the tissue paper. It's not a failsafe trick, but most stems should become bolt upright. With poppies, if you are in a hurry and want them to open quickly, you can force them along a bit by removing their furry hoods.

Ranunculus – snap off any buds that grow lower down the stem, as you only want the focal flower head.

Rose and hydrangea – these have woody stems, so it is a good idea to give them a vertical snip up the base of the stem to encourage them to drink – 5cm (2in) or so will suffice. Roses are most beautiful when fully blown and open. To aid this, keep them in warm water, remembering to recut the stems first. For a quick fix, and in moments of rose-opening desperation, blow sharply into the centre of the rose to puff up the petals. I've found the quickest and least painful way to remove thorns and prickly leaves is to use a foliage stripper, as the plastic gives your hand a bit of protection and will remove the majority. You can then go back in with scissors and snip out any stubborn thorns. Petal pick the flower head, taking care to remove the thicker guard petals to encourage the bloom to open.

Tulip – because of their soft stems and heavy heads, these can become quite droopy. Again, I personally don't mind this as I like the flowers to do their own thing and have a bit of character, but if you want them to stay straight, wrap them tightly in tissue paper and stand in deep water for at least two hours. Like anemones, tulips keep growing after they have been cut, so bear this in mind when including them in your arrangements.

Foliage

Approach foliage in the same way as flowers, taking care to ensure that any leaves that fall below the water line are removed. When it comes to the architectural foliage and branches such as oak, beech and birch, think about what you are using it for. If it's for a smaller vase arrangement, snip it down into more manageable pieces; you can get several pieces from one branch. If it is for a large installation and you want it to give your arrangement form, keep the pieces tall and lofty. Edit out anything that looks scruffy or too heavy. I tend to spend a bit of time snipping out individual leaves to get a lighter airiness to the branch.

Chapter I

Everyday

♥

'Flowers are part of the familiarity of home, of the everyday.'

Growing up we always had flowers throughout the house: celestial clouds of starburst lilies (my mum's absolute favourite) would be massed in the hallway, filling the entrance with a punch of perfume. Spring bulbs, usually grape hyacinths, would be potted in old planters and positioned by the kitchen window, the warmth of the sun encouraging them to peep through their soily blankets. And in our bedrooms my sisters and I would always find a little bud vase of something delicate and sweet: freesia, garden roses and twisty sweet-pea tendrils are distinct in my memory. Flowers are part of the familiarity of home, of the everyday, and in some ways I think that encouraged my relaxed approach to floristry. Flowers should be part of the tapestry of your home and your life.

In part it might be out of nostalgia that I have always been so passionate about having flowers in my own homes. For me, as my mum always says, a house just isn't a home without flowers. Even when I was at university living in grotty student digs on the Strand in London (trust me, this location sounds far more glamorous than it was), I always had flowers in the room. Nothing fancy, maybe just a little glass of daffodils, whatever was cheap, cheerful and seasonal, as a comfort in an unfamiliar world. Ultimately, there is nothing that will lift your mood and environment more quickly or successfully than beautiful blooms.

While I intrepidly made my way into the working world and through various rented shoeboxes across London, I was consistent about the presence of flowers wherever I laid my head. In my early twenties, when working in fashion, I was all about white flowers – I thought this was just *so* chic. But, as I hope you can see, I have now fully embraced the wonderful profusion of colours that nature has to offer!

Everyday flowers allow you to experiment with texture and pattern without committing to a whole new interior scheme, which is ideal if you are as indecisive as I sometimes am! Follow your heart when choosing your blooms; there is no point using a flower that you don't like, but you will undoubtedly make new blossom buddies as you go along.

Life is often so fast-paced that we can fly through days, weeks, months and even years without having the opportunity to stop and take a breath. Everything is instantaneous and immediate, so I feel passionately that introducing flowers into the home reaffirms presence – who we are and the world we are so fortunate to live in. Flowers remind us to live in the moment; they are temporary, but by embracing them in our everyday lives we get to enjoy the beauty of their transience.

The recipes in this chapter are simple and approachable. I want to encourage you to embrace the act of arranging flowers; it is rare to be able to craft something with your hands, and there is nothing more pride-inducing than creating something gorgeous that you and anyone who enters your home can enjoy.

Bottles, Jam Jars & Bud Vases

I wanted the first recipe in this book to be something I believe anyone can complete without getting stressed or worried that the flowers don't look 'right'. This is pretty much foolproof floristry.

The beauty of arranging flowers in this way is that they *will* look informal, by the very nature of the vessels – washed-out old bottles and jam jars, with the odd pretty bud vase picked up along the way. I got most of mine from Golborne or Kempton markets or charity shops on my travels. I do find it hard to resist a rummage in a charity shop – you never know what treasures you might discover!

I love dotting these dinky arrangements around the flat, on the entrance table where I leave my keys, maybe one by the soap in the kitchen so there's something pretty to look at when I'm doing the washing up, or clustered on the kitchen table for a casual centrepiece.

The informality of this arrangement, and the fact that you don't need *loads* of flowers, means that you could quickly rustle up a display with a couple of bunches from your local florist or supermarket, or, if you're lucky enough to have a garden, snippets of homegrown blooms.

Ingredients

· Selection of bottles, jam jars and bud vases. I like having different heights, shapes and sizes, but work with what you have – old or new, as long as they can hold water they will do the job

Foliage & flowers

· Foliage – Eucalyptus, Hebe, Olive, Rosemary, Variegated *Pittosporum*

· Flowers – Astrantia, Daffodil, *Genista*, Hellebore, Icelandic poppy, *Lisianthus*, Miranda rose (David Austin), *Prunus* blossom, sweet-pea flowers and tendrils

1. Gather your bottles, jam jars and bud vases and fill them three-quarters with cold water. Start by adding a sprig or two of foliage to each vessel, varying the height and type.

2. I always start by adding the tallest flowers. These will give a lightness to the arrangements, so keep the length where possible (even if it initially looks absurd). Next add the babes, the big-headed flowers. Keep some tall and cut some super-short so the heads just peep out.

3. Now go in with your dainty, wispy flourishes. Here the twisty curlicues of sweet-pea tendrils give a relaxed feel to the assortment.

Dinky Posy in a Vase

This recipe uses similar ingredients to the Bottles, Jam Jars & Bud Vases (see p. 26), but instead of splitting the ingredients up we are combining them into one gorgeous posy to nestle somewhere special.

I love to have an arrangement like this in the bedroom. There's something heavenly about having a small, scented cluster of blooms on your bedside table – and I truly think your dreams are sweeter when you're inhaling the soft perfumes of flowers beside your pillow.

(see p. 26)

Ingredients

· Small vase – I've used a cut-glass footed vase as I love the grandeur it gives to the arrangement

Foliage & flowers

· Foliage – Eucalyptus, Hebe, Olive, Rosemary, Variegated *Pittosporum*

· Flowers – Butterfly *Ranunculus*, 'Caramel Antike' rose, Cloni *Ranunculus*, 'Duchesse de Nemours' peony, *Lisianthus*, stocks, sweet-pea flowers and tendrils, white lilac

1. Begin by adding the foliage piece by piece, criss-crossing the stems in the water. Turn the vase as you add so that there is an even distribution. You want to create a stable framework using the foliage stems, so that the flowers (who, let's not forget, are the stars of the show) will have a cosy nest to settle into.

2. Once almost all the foliage is in, add pockets of the filler flowers. Here I have used *Lisianthus* and lilac. These flowers break up the density of the foliage and will act as a pretty backdrop against which the babes can sing!

3. Now add the big-headed babes, grouping them in twos and threes so that they look as they would growing in a garden, as I have done here with the Cloni *Ranunculus*. If this arrangement is for your bedside table, you will want to be able to see flowers from above as well as around the sides.

4. To finish, add some playful flourishes to stop the arrangement from looking too formal. Here I used dancing Butterfly *Ranunculus* and sweet-pea tendrils to add volume while softening the overall look.

Kitchen Blooms in a Jug

I feel particularly strongly that a house isn't a home without flowers in the kitchen. I always seem to gravitate towards the kitchen in anyone's house, especially my own, and my kitchen table is the centre of my world. If I'm doing flowers for my home I will do it there; if not, I will be found there writing and managing all the glorious emails and admin that comes with running your own business, and at the end of a long day I love nothing more than sitting down for a glass of something ice-cold and sparkly and a home-cooked supper.

I will be honest with you: when you are working with flowers as part of your 'day job', more often than not it's the last thing you want to be faffing with in your spare time. So, to ensure that this is a no-excuses weekly ritual, I've found a super-quick method that takes no more than five minutes from start to finish, and can be achieved with a couple of bunches picked up at the supermarket alongside the weekly shop. Speed floristry at its finest!

Ingredients

· Jug – ceramic, porcelain or earthenware (avoid glass if possible, as I find having the stems on display takes away from the blooms in something this simple – you want the blooms to be enhanced and punch out of the vessel)

Flowers

One type, preferably in a single colour, and whatever is in season. This is a very simple arrangement, so make sure you have plenty of stems; you want it to feel lavish and abundant. It depends on the size of your jug and the type of flower, but I would suggest anywhere between 20 and 50 stems.

· Flowers – I used Italian anemones

1. Bunch the flowers together in your hand (there is no need for this to be a pretty sight). Roughly arrange how you would like the flowers to fall in the vase. Think about how they would grow in a garden, so vary heights and directions, twisting some outwards and pulling other stems lower.

2. With the blooms still in your hand, measure against the jug. You want some of the flower heads to nestle against the jug lip, and some to reach up taller to give interest. Trim the stems accordingly.

3. Place flowers in vase, and ta-da! Weekly flowers in lightning speed.

Dried Flower Arrangement

As much as I am hoping to encourage you to bring lush fresh flowers into your life and home, I am a huge fan of dried flowers, too. I have bundles of papery hydrangea heads all over my place, as they are a great way of adding interest and texture to your interior without the need to replenish them constantly.

I buy British hydrangea in the autumn and dry them in their vase. Fill with water as usual and leave the arrangement to dry out naturally over time (the water will evaporate). Other flowers that you can try drying – although I have had mixed success – are: gypsophila, larkspur, *Nigella*, roses, sea holly, statice and strawflower. Seed heads and some foliage can look seriously chic, too; try angelica, grasses and poppy heads.

If you have the luxury of somewhere dark and warm to hang the blooms upside down – ideally a utility room or airing cupboard – you can tightly bind groupings of flowers using elastic bands, hang them for a few weeks to air-dry, and arrange them afterwards. The colours will fade to divine soft shades, like well-loved worn linens.

Ingredients

· Vase. I find opaque vessels work best, such as ceramic jugs or pots

Flowers

· Flowers – British hydrangea

♥ Tip — Potpourri

To create gorgeous homemade potpourri, simply scatter petals and flower heads on a big tray, sprinkle with silica gel and leave to dry for about a week. Throw the dried flowers into a plastic bag with some of your favourite essential oils and leave to infuse for a few hours. It makes a lovely house-warming present, and it's fabulous to have in the home, too; I have little pinch pots of it all around the flat, as I love having fragrance but can't always justify lighting expensive scented candles when it's a simple working-from-home day! The potpourri releases a gentle, heavenly background fragrance.

In a Pickle

This might be edging slightly out of the everyday, for when you're feeling a bit more fancy or ready to add a little razzmatazz to the working week. Don't be intimated by the size of this arrangement, though. Just imagine that this is a hulking great jam jar – the principles are the same, but the outcome is on a whole new scale.

Take your time when making this, and don't be afraid to go BIG (if your home allows it). This is my go-to arrangement to pop in the middle of the coffee table – much to my boyfriend's chagrin, as it will almost certainly block his view of the television. But hey-ho, we all have to compromise somewhere, and what's not to love about a lush pickle jar of joy?

Before starting, consider where the jar will be positioned. If it is going against a wall, focus the blooms at the front of the arrangement, but if it's destined for the middle of a table, make sure you have something interesting to look at all the way round, including a few blooms nestled deep in the centre.

Ingredients

· Large pickle jar

Foliage & flowers

· Foliage – Beech, British eucalyptus, *Cocculus*, dried grass, Pistache, Quince blossom, *Spirea*, *Thlaspi*, Winter honeysuckle

· Flowers – *Daucus*, Delphinium, *Exochorda* (also known as 'magical springtime', if you can believe it!), *Genista*, Larkspur, *Lisianthus*, *Moluccella*, Pink tuberose, 'Quicksand' rose, Sea lavender, Snapdragon

♥ Tip — Pickle jars

I love using vintage pickle jars because the glass has a wonderful mottled quality and I feel they have real history. They are also remarkably robust, which is always a good thing for a clumsy florist like me. I picked up a crate of them at Kempton Market years ago, and have added to my collection along the way with market finds.

You can get great reproduction, old-fashioned-looking pickle jars, too. What you're ideally looking for is a large vessel that will be able to take the height and weight of lofty foliage, but with a narrowing at the neck so you don't have to spend a fortune filling it. If you don't have a pickle jar, a big old water jug will also work.

1. Start by adding the more architectural foliage branches. Review each stem before you put it in the vase, turn it around and see which angle is the most pleasing – the blossom I used had a natural sweeping curve, so I used it on the left-hand side to add asymmetry to the design. The *Spirea* adds a light airiness to this initial step.

2. Fill in the spaces between the branches with lighter foliage. Here I have used beech and eucalyptus to bulk out some of the space between the branches. The *Thlaspi* adds a peppering of zingy green and complements the *Spirea* buds.

3. Once all the foliage is in place, you can add some of the taller blooms. Use their height to add drama and movement to the arrangement. I love the way the *Moluccella* dances and twists towards the light, with its pretty scallop-edged flower. The candyfloss-coloured snapdragons add pops of colour, while the *Genista* gives a sugary-sweet dusting of powder pink.

4. Finally add the remaining flowers. The 'Quicksand' roses were the perfect shade to unite the white delphinium and magical springtime with the snapdragons and *Genista*, so I nestled them in the heart of the arrangement. I then added a few lofty stems of *Daucus* and dried grasses to give a meadow feel to the pickle jar.

Candlestick with a Floral Touch

I discovered this idea when faced with having to choose between candlelight and flowers on the table at a supper I was hosting. The table was already a squeeze, considering the number of people I had invited, and I was serving giant sharing platters of food. I realized there was only space for either the candlesticks *or* the flowers, so I decided to combine the two! I quickly soaked some little cubes of floral foam and taped them to the stick, and repurposed the blooms I had already cut down for the bud vases I'd hoped to dot on the table. They looked super-pretty and were the perfect solution to a potential dinner-party disaster.

This is a brilliant way to use up any flowers with stems that have snapped and are too short to be used in other arrangements. The beauty of it is that you don't need masses of flowers, just a whisper of florals to create something unusual to elevate an otherwise simple supper.

Of course, if you wanted to use these in a more formal way you could have a row of floral candlesticks running the length of the table. I love to use the very tall tapered candles, as they look so elegant. In between the candlesticks place beautiful bud vases or vases of blooms with tealights in decorative glasses, for an extra level of lighting across the table.

Ingredients

· Candlestick(s) – as many as you wish to use

· Block of floral foam, soaked (see guidelines on p. 16)

· Knife – it doesn't need to be sharp; a table knife is fine

· Florist pot tape

Foliage & flowers

· Foliage – Asparagus fern, Leatherleaf fern, *Senecio*, Viburnum

· Flowers – Carnation, Carnival *Ranunculus*, Cloni *Ranunculus*, Heather, Waxflower

♥ **Tip – Safety first**

Take care to blow the candle out before it burns down to the flowers. We don't want anything to get singed!

♥ **Tip – Foam-free**

Rather than using floral foam, you could attach a small thimble of water to the candlestick using pot tape. Use it like a little vase and pop flowers and foliage directly into it.

1. Cut a square of floral foam for each candlestick, using a knife. Gauge the size of the squares based on the size of each candlestick; you don't want anything that will be too heavy and cause the candlestick to fall over.

2. Attach the foam to the candlestick with small pieces of florist pot tape.

3. Begin by inserting the foliage, remembering to cut the stem at a sharp angle before pushing it into the foam.

4. Use the foliage to completely hide the mechanics of the arrangement. Nobody wants to see foam or pot tape.

5. Once you have a good covering, add the flowers, trimming stems if necessary. You want to create a tight formation of blooms around the candlestick to keep everything in proportion.

Floral Wreath

I believe wreaths should be enjoyed all year round, not just at Christmas. Why reserve them for the festive season when you can festoon your doors with them 'just because'? The circular nature of a wreath symbolizes unity and inclusion, lovely sentiments to be reminded of when you reach your front door.

In spring why not create a branch base by winding supple willow or other bendy branches into a nest, and stud it with cherry and apple blossom? Summer brings a glorious glut of blooms, so go maximal – imagine how gorgeous a wreath completely made up of peonies would look! You could use several different varieties to create an ombre effect of pinks, or stick with one type for serious impact.

Fallen autumn leaves provide the most amazing colours, from golden yellows through to burnt umber. I would suggest using exclusively dried elements (no moss needed), and simply binding twigs, branches and leaves directly to the wreath base. For a harvest nod you could wire pretty fruit and vegetables to the wreath – baby pumpkins, ripe plums and figs spring to mind.

Of course, winter means Christmas and all the fir, pinecones, holly and ivy, lichen branches and crab apples you can possibly cram on to your wreath. But for a super-chic alternative, you could bury small pots of trailing ivy and hellebore in the moss and twist and trail the foliage around, keeping things in place with small twists of wire if necessary.

Ingredients

· Bind wire

· Wire wreath ring. These come in a range of sizes, from 20cm to 50cm (7–20in). I tend to go for something around 25–30cm (9–11in), but if you're feeling brave, go bigger

· Moss

· Florist test tubes (if adding flowers)

Foliage & flowers

Take care to remove any gnarly, ugly bits and divide into bundles of 3–5 stems.

· Foliage – Berried eucalyptus, English eucalyptus, Heather, Olive

· Flowers (optional) – Chrysanthemum, Freesia, *Genista*, Lilac, *Prunus* blossom

♥ Tip – Command hooks

If you are reluctant to damage your door by hammering a nail into it, why not use a stick-on Command hook? They are really easy to install and you can remove them when you take the wreath down.

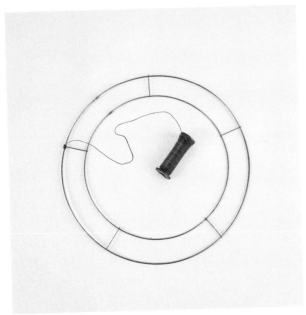

1. Attach the bind wire to the wreath ring by twisting it around the frame a few times. Keep the wire on the spool.

2. Take a large handful of moss and squish it on to the wreath ring. You want this to be nice and springy, so don't scrimp on the handful! Secure the moss against the wreath ring by wrapping the wire around it a few times.

3. Continue adding moss to the wreath, working around until it is completely covered, keeping the wire on the spool.

4. Place the first foliage bundle on to the mossy wreath, pushing the stems slightly into the moss as you do so (the moss holds water, so will keep your wreath looking fresh). Secure with the bind wire, which should still be attached to the mossy base.

5. Keep adding bundles of foliage, each overlapping the one before to cover the stems and your wiring.

6. Repeat until the whole base is covered in foliage. At this point I usually put it on the floor and get a good bird's-eye perspective of the design. If necessary, add extra foliage and fluff up any parts of the wreath that look a little sparse.

7. You could happily leave the wreath as it is, all green and gorgeous, but if you fancy adding some florals to make it extra-special, now is the time. Some flowers can be added directly into the wreath, as I have done here with the *Genista* – simply cut the stem at a sharp angle and spear it through the foliage into the mossy base.

Others will last longer if they are in water, so I use florist test tubes for those blooms. Simply fill with water, pop the stem in and wedge into the foliage. It should be dense enough that the test tube will hold itself in there, but if you're worried it might slip out, reinforce with wire.

Chapter II

Entertaining

♥

'Tablescapes with beautiful blooms for impressing your guests.'

It isn't all about the aesthetic when it comes to being a gracious host. Delicious food and something lovely to drink are essential, as is riveting conversation and an interesting mix of guests, but I firmly believe that if you put the effort into setting the scene, the rest of the celebration will swing along in just the way you hope. Seeing a table festooned with blooms, gorgeous linens and coloured glassware is sure to make even the most unobservant curmudgeon gleeful.

This chapter is all about hosting during the day, and I have to admit that I am a sucker for this sort of event. The kind of get-togethers I'm envisaging for this chapter are dreamy daytime gatherings bathed in dappled sunlight. It's low-key because it's daytime, but you still want to show off a bit and impress your guests with your thoughtfulness and attention to detail. I'm thinking special birthday breakfasts, best-mate brunches, long, lazy lunches, al fresco tea parties and everything in between ... but of course you could quite happily use these arrangements for suppers, evening cocktails or full-on raves if you wish!

I am lucky enough to have my birthday in June, and every year I use this opportunity to create a bounty of blooms just for me. Well, not just for me; I invite all my friends and family around for a gathering, and I tend to opt for a late lunch that can linger into the early evening. One year there was a glut of peonies at the flower market I couldn't resist, so I bought them in every shade and type imaginable. I had armfuls of them. I can't remember exactly how many stems, but there must have been over a hundred. I created a sea of peonies all down the table in low vases, and was lucky enough that the weather was warm and they all popped open just in time for my birthday. Peony perfection!

When it comes to flowers, soft, free and gentle works well for these sorts of event – you don't want anything too high-drama for the daytime. Subtlety is key, despite the effort that might go into creating a dream tablescape. One of the tricks of being the perfect host is to act nonchalant. There has been a huge resurgence in the popularity of flowers as everyday decoration, becoming part of your interior, and when you have visitors there is no reason not to channel your inner peacock and take the chance to show off. After all, your home is an extension of you, your personality and your style. I always seize the opportunity to put in that extra effort with floral flourishes when I know I have guests coming over.

Working on the florals is the reward for having finished all the hard work ahead of your guests arriving. Your home has been swept and now sparkles, linen is laid, the food is prepped, there is something heavenly to drink upon arrival, and cushions are fluffed and welcoming. All you have to do now is take a quick time out to be creative and make something natural and beautiful to set the scene for your shindig. At the very least it will look pretty, and at its best it should make your guests swoon and sigh. Have faith that the effort you have put into the flowers will transform your event from a basic brunch into something stop-in-your-tracks Instagram-worthy (the ultimate goal for a host).

Floral Place Settings

A table plan gives direction and avoids the awkward shuffling around the table without anyone knowing where best to place themselves. It also means that you can encourage your guests to meet new people and socialize with those they aren't familiar with. Place settings are the sweetest way to signal a table plan. They not only indicate where you would like everybody to sit, but are also a lovely memento for your guests to take away with them.

These posies are perfect for using up tiny stems or snapped heads that are too short for other arrangements. And don't forget to include dried elements, such as strawflower and grasses to give texture and interest. I would suggest making these the day before, if you are hosting a breakfast or brunch, or first thing in the morning if you're hosting lunch.

Ingredients

· Short vases or bottles (for temporary storage, not display)

· Florist tape

· Ribbon

· Card and writing equipment

Foliage & flowers

· Foliage – Dried heather, Rosemary, *Senecio*, Waxflower

· Flowers – Butterfly *Ranunculus*, Clematis, *Oxypetalum*, *Ranunculus*, Scabious

♥ Tip — Choose hardy stems

Although flowers don't love being out of water, if you give them a good drink beforehand they should last for the duration of your event. Pick hardy stems: things like *Dianthus*, roses, rosebuds and sweet william are very robust.

1. Separate the foliage and flowers into little groups, one for each guest, and gather the foliage for each one. Place stems vertically, to create a stable background.

2. When you have a lovely, full bundle of foliage, add flower stems to fluff out the posy. Place the stems on top of the foliage and hold them in place by pinching between your thumb and forefinger.

3. Now add your babes. I like to nestle one close to where the posy will be tied, so it peeps out over the ribbon.

4. Secure the posy with florist tape. Stretch the tape as you twist it around the stems, to get a tight bind point. I use florist tape because it's waterproof, so that if you are going to stand the posies in water before your event it will remain intact. I also love that it is green so blends in with the stems.

5. Carefully stand the miniature posy in a vase or bottle filled with water to keep them hydrated. Then just before your guests arrive, dry them off on a kitchen towel and tie a length of ribbon around each posy, covering the florist tape as you do so. Finish with a handwritten card and position at the table.

Flowery Cake Stand

There is nothing more glorious than a cake resplendently bejewelled with fresh flowers, a decoration no longer reserved for wedding cakes. This is the perfect way to add petalled polish to cakes for all manner of celebration – birthdays, engagements or just a good old-fashioned tea party.

This design will create a perfumed plume of blooms at the base of your cake. If you can, use moss rather than floral foam in a design like this. Although it will not be touching your cake, it is in very close proximity to it, so it's best to keep everything fresh and natural.

Ingredients

· Large cake stand (this will be the base that holds the florals)

· Smaller cake stand or footed plate (this will stand on top of the larger stand, and hold the cake). I like to use clear glass cake stands to create a magical floating pillow of petals for the cake to stand on

· Florist adhesive tack

· Chicken wire

· Sharp snips/wire cutters

· Moss

· Gardening gloves

· Florist pot tape

Foliage & flowers

· Foliage – Asparagus fern, Eucalyptus, Leatherleaf fern

· Flowers – Antique rose, 'Carbonara' gerbera, Cloni *Ranunculus*, 'Golden Mustard' rose, Pon Pon *Ranunculus*, 'Quicksand' rose

♥ **Tip** — Blossoming tea

Warm up an autumn or winter gathering with theatrical blossoming teas, which are fun to serve in glass teapots and teacups. Made using green tea leaves handsewn together with flower buds, these are a feat of craftsmanship as well as caffeine! Delight in the surprise of your guests as the 'tea ball' unfurls to reveal a colourful chrysanthemum, marigold or jasmine flower.

1. Place the small cake stand on top of the larger one. As an extra precaution, use a little florist adhesive tack to stick them together. Carefully cut a piece of chicken wire, determining the length required by measuring the circumference of the larger cake stand. The height of the piece should be about twice the height between the two cake platforms.

2. Take thick bundles of moss and place them on the chicken wire. Roll the chicken wire tightly around the moss and secure by folding the wire ends back on themselves. Do wear gardening gloves for this.

3. Wedge the moss roll into the space between the two cake stands. This is where the flowers will be inserted. It should be wedged enough that it feels secure, but if necessary use florist pot tape to reinforce it.

4. Add the foliage, cutting the stems at a sharp angle and pushing them directly into the moss. I've added feathery ferns to give a slightly untamed garden look.

5. When you have a good covering of foliage, add the flowers. I wanted to keep this looking really luxurious, befitting a special garden party, so I've grouped the large flower heads together.

6. Completely cover the moss with blooms. I worked with a sugary palette of powdery pink, blush and golden caramel to complement the wonderful cake.

Floral Garnishes

To continue your floribunda feast, I would strongly suggest that the theme creep into the refreshments. In spring and summer, serve delicious cordials with these floral ice cubes. Although they are a little fiddly to create, they add a petalled prettiness to al fresco drinks. I serve sparkling elderflower cordial and fresh raspberries for a delicious pick-me-up.

If you are a host/hostess with the mostest but without the mostest amount of time, fill the ice-cube tray with distilled water, pop the flowers in and allow the cubes to freeze in one go. The flowers might all cluster in one part of the ice cube, but it will still be a charming addition to any drink.

Ingredients

· Distilled water – this keeps the ice crystals clear

· Ice-cube tray

· Edible flowers, such as pansies, *Dianthus* or nasturtiums

Recipe

· Using distilled water, fill an ice-cube tray one-quarter full and pop it in the freezer. Once set, add a layer of edible flowers, top up with water until half full and return to the freezer. Allow to set and repeat the process for the final layer of flowers, topping the water up completely and returning for the final freeze. Adding the flowers in layers means the blooms are suspended throughout the transparent ice cube.

♥ Tip — Cake flowers

Why not try adding flowers to the cake itself? Do be careful about the types of flowers and plants you use, though, as some are harmful if ingested (for example, clematis and lily of the valley). If you use organic, edible flowers (I get mine from specialist suppliers), you can dress your cake directly. Either place the flowers on the fresh icing or push the stems into the cake itself.

Table Garland

This is a brilliant way to dress your table when you wish to keep flowers to a minimum, but still want to impress.

My favourite sort of garland is light and uses fine foliage such as passion flower vine, sweet-pea tendrils, trailing jasmine and asparagus fern. The delicacy of these garlands lends itself to a special intimate supper and looks extremely pretty when they are laid on printed linen tablecloths and twisted around candles. For this kind of garland, use longer lengths of foliage and connect the stems with tiny twists of wire, rather like a long, loopy daisy chain.

For something bigger – whether for a table, banister, door frame or mantelpiece – this recipe is ideal, and will make a lusciously bushy garland. Decide where you are going to install your garland and measure the space. If it is to decorate a table, simply measure the length of the table. For any other installations, use string to measure out the ideal length. For example, use it to plan how many times you would like to wind it around a banister, and when you have planned it, measure the string and make a garland to this length.

Garlands are particularly popular during the Christmas season, when I would recommend using varieties of fir and eucalyptus (which give off an incredible festive scent). Rather than studding the foliage with fresh flowers, decorate with pinecones, peppercorn berries and dried slices of orange and lime.

Ingredients

· Florist bind wire

· Florist test tubes (if using flowers)

Foliage

I usually allow three bunches of foliage for every metre (3ft) of garland. I like to use different varieties for a mixture of tones and texture, so I suggest using at least three different types.

· Foliage – Asparagus fern, Berried ivy, Leatherleaf fern, Soft *Ruscus*, Viburnum

♥ **Tip** — Florist test tubes

If you wish, add flowers to the garland using florist test tubes. Fill with water and pop the stem into the vial, then nestle each directly into the foliage garland. The foliage should be dense enough to keep the test tube in place. Take care to conceal the tube, either by ruffling the foliage around it or by hiding it with small pieces of moss.

1. Make little bundles of mixed foliage and prepare the florist bind wire by making a loop at the end. The loop makes it easier to handle the garland, and is useful if you want to hang it or secure it to a banister. Keep the wire on the reel.

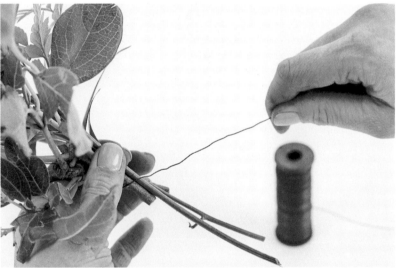

2. Begin by taking the first bundle in your left hand and secure by winding the florist wire around the stems. Wind around a good few times to make sure it is bound tightly.

3. Do not cut the wire; keep it on the reel throughout to create a strong and stable base for your garland.

4. Lay the next bundle of foliage on top of the first, angling it slightly as you do and concealing the stems of the first bundle. Using the wire that is still on the reel, secure the second bundle with a few strong twists of the wire.

5. Continue to add foliage bundles in the same way. The garland will gradually grow longer, so do persevere!

6. Once all the foliage has been used up and you have the desired length of garland, cut the wire and wrap at the end to secure. See tip on using florist test tubes to add flowers if desired.

Garlands can be made a day or two in advance. Just make sure you give yours a good dousing of water from a florist spray bottle and leave it wrapped in a parcel of cellophane or a big bin bag, preferably outside if it's not freezing, or in a cool, dry place.

Compote Arrangement

Not to be confused with the delicious sticky, fruity syrup you are probably more familiar with, a compote is a footed vessel that was traditionally used for serving fruit or nuts, and is a lovely thing to arrange flowers in.

This sort of arrangement looks very special because you don't see any of the 'mechanics' – no distracting cut stems, no water – this is a celebration of blooms! Generally speaking, a compote should have a central support so that the arrangement is elevated, but you can just as easily use the same technique in a bowl.

Compote arrangements can be used as a centrepiece on the table. They're great for brunches or big Sunday lunches when you want to cram as much food on the table as possible! If yours is to be used as a centrepiece, think about the design 'in the round', so there is something lovely to see from all angles (this is when lazy Susan leaps into action!). However, compote arrangements work just as well on a side table, bookshelf or mantelpiece, in which case you need only think about the front of the design.

Ingredients

· Compote vessel. This can be pretty much any material – glass, metal, ceramic – but ideally should have a footed base

· Chicken wire

· Florist tape

· Lazy Susan (optional)

Foliage & flowers

· Foliage – Asparagus fern, Berried ivy, Guelder rose, *Senecio*, Soft *Ruscus*

· Flowers – Butterfly *Ranunculus*, 'Café Latte' rose, Carnival *Ranunculus*, Cloni *Ranunculus*, Daffodil, *Daucus*, Forget-me-not, Poppy, 'Sarah Bernhardt' peony

♥ **Tip** — A centrepiece

If your compote will be seen from all angles, for instance in the middle of a table, approach the arrangement in phases. Begin with the front 'face', working through the steps until that side of the arrangement is finished. Then turn the compote and repeat the process on the next few 'faces' until you have come full circle. I find it much easier to break it down like this, as it can be overwhelming trying to get the overall design right from the outset.

1. Measure a small section of chicken wire, enough to fit like a ball into your compote vessel. This will provide a latticed support for the flowers. Secure the chicken wire using florist tape. Fill the compote with clean, cold water and, if you're using one, pop the compote on your lazy Susan. I always use one, and I think it's incredibly unfair to call Susan lazy: she does all the spinning around so you don't have to!

2. Start by adding some foliage to get the basic structure of your arrangement. Bear in mind where you will be positioning the arrangement and snip stems accordingly – always remember you can snip things shorter but can't add height once it's gone, so err on the side of caution! Here I added springy guelder rose as my starting point; the sherbet-green pom-poms immediately give a good structure.

3. Fill in with more foliage, creating a fullness that fans out from the compote. Here I have gone for quite a balanced distribution, with some trailing asparagus fern to soften one side.

4. Start by adding the smaller flowers, keeping the stems long and lofty. I have concentrated on adding these to the left-hand side for asymmetry, to prevent the arrangement from looking too perfect.

5. Finally, add your showstopper blooms to give the compote a punch! Here I have clustered a 'Café Latte' rose deep in next to an open Cloni and Carnival *Ranunculus*. The coppery tones of the rose work beautifully next to the salmon-pink *Ranunculus*. I've kept these close to the base of the arrangement, filling the space between the taller blooms and the foliage around the lip of the compote.

To balance the lower stems, I have added a buttery-yellow poppy and a fully blown peony above, to keep the eye moving around the arrangement, and some *Daucus* just nudging outwards on the right-hand side.

Showstopper Urn

This could just as easily be called the Show-Off Urn, because it will wow your guests. Think of it as the floral equivalent of serving a huge, perfectly risen soufflé – major gasps all round. I would save it for a special bash, when you have guests whom you really want to impress.

Its grandeur belies the fact that it is actually rather simple to make. You need the bravery and boldness of In a Pickle (p. 40) combined with the slightly more technical aspect of the Compote Arrangement (p. 74).

An urn makes a fabulous statement, but its size means that you need to give some thought to the positioning. The arrangement can become quite large, so I would suggest placing it against a wall, be it on a desk or side table in a nook of the room, or in a corner of the kitchen counter, so that it doesn't eat into the room too much.

If you can, put the urn in its final position before you start. These huge arrangements become heavy and tricky to manoeuvre once they are blossomed up.

Ingredients

· Urn. Be it from a garden centre or salvage yard, the most important thing is that it is totally watertight

· Cellophane or black plastic bin bag

· Chicken wire

· Sharp snips/wire cutters

· Florist pot tape

Foliage & flowers

This is a large arrangement, so you really need to think about proportion and go for stems that will give you impact. I would weight the distribution in favour of foliage. This is where you want to get the loppers out in the garden if you can! Leafy, structural foliage is perfect.

· Foliage – Beech, blossom, Cotoneaster, Guelder rose, *Senecio*, Soft *Ruscus*, *Spirea*, *Thlaspi*

· Flowers – 'Bombastic' spray rose, Butterfly *Ranunculus*, 'Carbonara' gerbera, Clematis, *Daucus*, Delphinium, *Exochorda* (magical springtime), 'Keira' rose (David Austin), *Lisianthus*, *Moluccella*, Pink tuberose, 'Sarah Bernhardt' peony, Scabious, Sea lavender, Snapdragon, 'Vuvuzela' rose, Waxflower

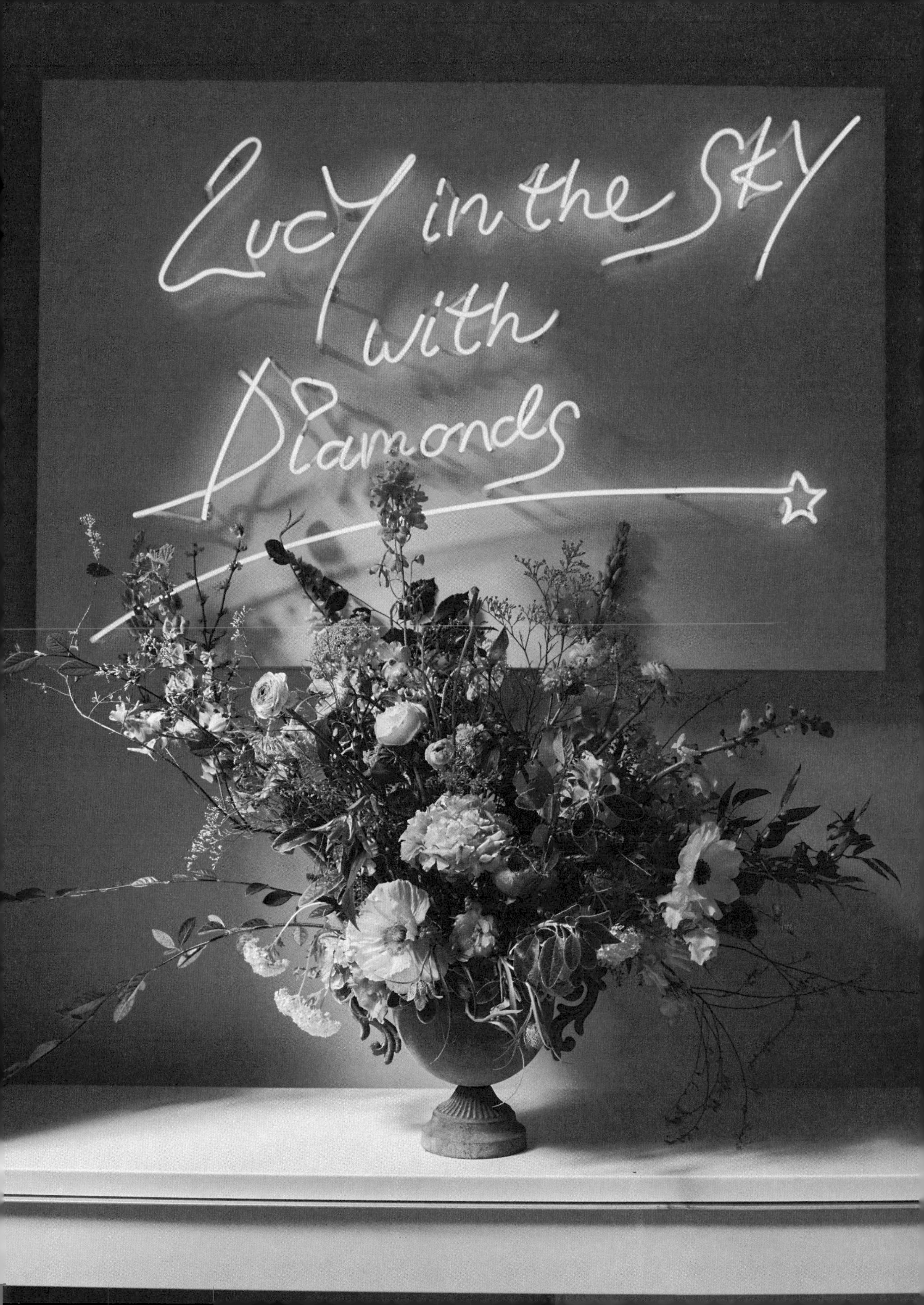
Lucy in the sky
with
Diamonds

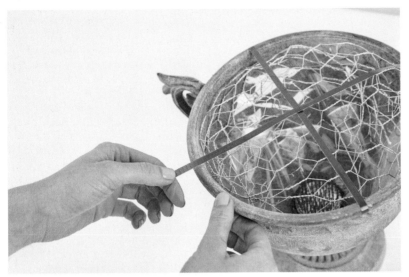

1. Start by making sure your urn is watertight. Even if it is new, I would always line it with cellophane just to be on the safe side. Cut a large square of chicken wire, bigger than the top of the urn, and fold it into a roundish pillow shape. Push it into the top of the urn, crushing it in so it fills the opening but still leaves room for stems to be pushed through. Secure the chicken wire with lengths of pot tape across the top. Once it is in position, fill the urn with clean, cold water.

2. Add structural, branchy foliage to get the basic shape of your arrangement. The chicken wire will support these stems, but they may move as you add to the arrangement. Don't be alarmed by this; be confident – you can always tweak and move things around at the end. Here I have used the height of the foliage to their full potential, arching up and out of the urn.

3. Fill in the framework with the supporting foliage. Here I have created density using beech and soft *Ruscus*, while the *Thlaspi* offers a dainty smattering of tiny green bells throughout. You want the arrangement to have impact without being brutish, so edit out thick bits of foliage and keep it lightweight. Once you're happy with the initial structure, add some of the softer foliage to fill in the overall shape.

4. Begin adding the flowers. Here I wanted to get an overall sprinkling of colour, so I worked the pops of golden-yellow Butterfly *Ranunculus* at strategic points to make the eye travel around the composition. I kept most tall and snuck one or two in near the base of the arrangement. I followed it with sweet pink *Lisianthus* and clusters of waxflower, because I loved the peachy-pink tones against the yolky yellow.

5. Now it is time for the lovely leggy flowers – go tall to echo the heights of your tallest foliage. To stop the arrangement from getting too fan-like, I focused on adding these tall blooms on the left-hand side. Here I added a couple of *Moluccella*, some pink tuberose and some delphinium. Soften any gaps with filler flowers such as fluffy *Daucus* and wispy sea lavender.

6. Finally it is time to add the babes. I love using big, round-headed flowers in arrangements like this as I think it grounds the piece. Keep these flowers in the bottom third of the arrangement, putting some close to the rim of the urn, and others nodding beside them, as I have done here with the spray roses and the peony.

Chapter III

'Flowers are ephemeral, but the sentiment with which they are delivered is eternal.'

It's all very well ensconcing yourself in your home filled with flowers, but one of the most satisfying things to do with them is to share them. By their very nature flowers are ephemeral, but the sentiment with which they are delivered is eternal. Flowers are a physical representation of emotion: whether you are telling your best friend who lives on the other side of the country that you miss them, sending sympathy and thoughts to a loved one who has suffered loss, or sharing joy at good news, flowers can convey a myriad of emotions.

When I started my business I would deliver absolutely every bouquet myself. I would get up at dawn to hustle down to the flower market, rush back to the studio to spend the morning preparing, conditioning and arranging the blooms, then set off early afternoon to make the rounds either on my bicycle or in my trusty old Mini. Seeing someone peep round their door to discover an unexpected flower urchin on their doorstep is truly one of the best things about working with flowers. The usual response is beams of delight, although there have been the odd slightly surprised characters who enquire nervously, 'But who are they from?' I still try to do as many deliveries as I can myself, even if the schedule doesn't really allow it, because I love seeing flowers make people happy.

When you are sending cut flowers, whether as a bouquet or in a vase arrangement, always try to include something that smells lovely. My years of deliveries have proved to me that people have an almost primal reaction to bend their heads into a bouquet and take a good, deep sniff – we expect flowers to have perfume. Depending on the time of year, an ambrosial bloom might not be available, so include herbs or fragrant foliage instead.

If you really want to impress, you could explore floriography, the language of flowers. Flowers have carried meaning for thousands of years throughout Asia, Europe and the Middle East, but floriography was at its height during the prim and proper Victorian period in Britain. In a society where proper etiquette was expected and open conversation stifled, it enabled the discreet communication of secret messages. Each flower was endowed with a particular meaning, and single stems or groupings of stems would be sent according to the nature of the conversation. There were subtle nuances between meanings of the same flower. For example, a blood-red rose meant 'I love you', whereas a deep-red rose signified shame. I imagine it was quite easy to get wires (or should that be vines?) crossed!

Choosing Flowers for Bouquets

There are four key decisions I make when choosing which flowers to use for a bouquet.

1. Recipient
I like to think about the recipient and try to work out what makes them tick. If it's for a girlfriend I will probably make something I would love, probably all pinks, and hope that by default they will love it too. If it's for a guy I make it foliage-rich and keep to a tonal palette. If it's for my mum I go for something classic, with lots of whites, creams and blushes.

2. Colour
When choosing the colour palette, go with your heart and whatever you think your recipient will love. Bear in mind that the 'bridging' colour is often as important, if not more so, than your hero colours. Say you are working with cream and dark magenta – placed right next to each other these can jar, but if you bridge the palette with blush and mauve there is harmony.

Think also about the foliage you're using, and whether it complements the flowers. There are many different shades of leaf colour – from glaucous grey–blues through to acid yellow–limes and on to deep evergreens, and even darker reds and blacks. Consider foliage as your friend; it's cheaper to buy than flowers and will add a fullness to your arrangements that would be very expensive to achieve with flowers alone.

3. Texture
Perhaps because of my fashion background, I think of flowers almost as textiles or tapestry – you want a richness in the different textures. Instead of using only smooth, glossy-looking elements, add some dried grasses or seed heads, and perhaps some feathery foliage. You want to create interest and excitement for the eye.

4. Scent
We expect flowers to smell lovely, but the sad fact is that so many have been grown on a vast commercial scale that the fragrance has been bred out of them. Some of my favourite scented varieties are:

Garden roses (the dream), peonies (can be total heaven), lilac, stocks (peppery and tangy), chocolate cosmos (they really do smell like chocolate), clematis on the vine (this was a surprise, as the cut flower doesn't really smell), lily of the valley, tuberose (slightly divisive; you either love it or hate it), mock orange, honeysuckle (reminds me of home), freesia, hyacinth (beautiful, but can become overpowering in a small house), jasmine (probably one of my favourite smells), sweet pea (this is the smell I associate with summer), daffodil (the smell that conjures spring).

If you can't get any scented flowers, foliage will be your friend (again!) – eucalyptus, geranium, myrtle, *Monarda* (bergamot), rosemary, mint and sage all have divine fragrances in their own right.

Bouquet

Receiving flowers is one of life's simple pleasures – such a treat and all the sweeter if someone has gone to the trouble of personally making something with you in mind. I've had such fun writing out all the lovely, funny, poignant, moving and generally gorgeous things people say to one another when they are sending flowers. One of the best cards I've ever been asked to write simply said, 'Because it's Wednesday, and I love you.' So romantic.

To give a professional polish to your bouquet you can always spend an extra ten minutes wrapping it. If you'll be delivering it within an hour or so and you know the recipient will be able to put it in water straight away, leave it as it is with the stems exposed, swaddle it with layers of tissue and a thick piece of paper and tie with a ribbon.

If you have further to travel, it is best to give the flowers something to drink so that they look pretty and perky on arrival. Stand the bouquet on a square of cellophane and pick up each corner in turn, pulling them up to meet the bouquet and securing each with the hand holding the flowers. Fasten the cellophane-covered stems with twine or string before covering the wrapped bouquet with paper and securing that more beautifully with a ribbon. Then carefully trickle water into the centre of your bouquet. Stop when you have covered about an inch or so of the bottom of the stems. Make sure you keep it upright in transit to avoid spilling the water.

Ingredients

· Twine or string

· Wrapping (optional; see text on left)

Foliage & flowers

I like to make my bouquets quite foliage-heavy, as it is always a lot more affordable than flowers, adds a richness to the bouquet and provides a lush green background against which the flowers can sing. I normally use the ratio of two-thirds foliage to one-third flower.

· Foliage – Berried ivy, British eucalyptus, Camellia, Hebe

· Flowers – Astrantia, blossom, Butterfly *Ranunculus*, 'Caramel Antike' rose, 'Doctor Alexander Fleming' peony, *Genista*, Lilac, 'Raspberry Scoop' scabious, 'Secret Garden' rose, sweet-pea flowers and tendrils

1. Start with the foliage. Take a stem in your right hand and place it in your left hand, keeping it in place with a firm grip between your thumb and fingers. This will become your bind point, where you will tie off your bouquet. Take a second stem of foliage and place it at an angle across the first stem.

2. Repeat with a few more stems of foliage. Each time you add a new stem, turn the foliage in your hand, taking care to keep a tight grip around the bind point so that you are building the foliage up 'in the round'. Continue until you have used approximately 10 stems. Angling the stems will force them to create a strong and supportive spiral for your bushy foliage base.

3. Fluffy filler flowers such as lilac will provide texture, colour and intrigue without being the stars of the show. Slightly loosen the grip in your left hand (which is holding the foliage) and push the flower stem into the centre, angling it as you do to add to the spiral of stems.

4. Keep adding the filler flowers, varying the type of flower, and turning the bouquet in your hand. Here I have included *Genista*, rust-coloured Butterfly *Ranunculus* and astrantia, as each has different characteristics and adds depth to the texture of the bouquet.

5. Next, add your babes. You want these to have pride of place, so I usually insert one fairly centrally, as I have done here with the incredible 'Doctor Alexander Fleming' peony. Nestle a couple of other pretty blooms beside it to keep it company (here the whispers of sweet peas and their twisty tendrils are doing this just perfectly).

6. The tying of the bouquet can be a little fiddly because if you put it down without tying it you risk your masterpiece falling apart! There are several different ways of doing this, but this is the way I do it. Cut a length of string long enough that you will easily be able to wrap the bouquet a good few times. Take the end of the string in your left hand, using your pinky finger to hook on to it.

7. Clamp your little finger on to the string, and twist it around the bouquet. Turn the flowers upside down if you need more purchase or if your bouquet is particularly chubby.

8. Once you have twisted the string around the bouquet a few times, tie it in a tight knot and trim the string. Trim the stems so they are all one length and put the bouquet in water.

Little Vase Arrangement

This is the perfect gift to take to your host when you've been invited to stay for a weekend – whether it's the in-laws, friends or family. The flowers can be placed on the host's kitchen table or in the entrance hall, and everyone can enjoy them for the duration of the stay.

The beauty of taking them in a vase is three-fold: you don't have to worry about wrapping the arrangement, there is no faff or bother for your host to find a vase to put it in, and they get to keep the vase to use later. It's a winner!

I like to use small vases that have a narrow neck but can be packed with blooms. Anything too wide will slosh water around, and however you're travelling, nobody wants that.

Ingredients

· Small vase with a narrow neck

Foliage & flowers

· Foliage – *Pittosporum* (variegated and non-variegated), *Senecio*, Viburnum

· Flowers – Butterfly *Ranunculus*, Cloni *Ranunculus*, Hellebore, *Lisianthus*, Phlox, Snapdragon

♥ **Tip** — Flower names

In my very neatest handwriting I like to write down what is included in my little arrangement on a card luggage label and tie it around the neck of the vase, using a gorgeous ribbon to match the colour of the flowers. This sweet extra touch lets your host know exactly what beautiful blooms you have chosen for them.

1. Ensure your vase is clean and three-quarter fill it with cold water. Add the foliage first, creating a simple framework for the flowers to be popped into.

2. Begin to add flowers, keeping them in proportion with the foliage – nothing too tall. I love the sugary pinks of the phlox and the pale blush *Ranunculus*, but wanted a bit of contrast so I added the dark pink *Lisianthus* to give a pop.

3. Keep adding flowers until you have a petite but full arrangement. Avoid using
anything too tall, as it makes the arrangement trickier to transport. Even here
I have kept the taller flowers, like the snapdragon, short.

Pressed Flowers

I've always loved pressing flowers. I distinctly remember collecting little buds, interesting-looking weeds and tiny petals with my sisters when we were little, carefully placing them in one of those old-fashioned flower presses and waiting with bated breath, ever so patiently, for what seemed like months, for them to be transformed into delicate, papery husks.

Nowadays we can expedite the process, but you still need to allow a good week for them to dry out, so if you're planning on creating something with pressed flowers for your best friend's birthday, don't leave it until the day before.

The beauty of this recipe is that you don't need masses of blooms to make something special and lovely – in fact, the dinkier the better, as it adds to their delicacy. Avoid any flower or foliage with a thick or succulent stem. Cuttings that work best are perennial plants (plants that return year after year with blooms), herbs, ferns, leaves and even weed tendrils. It's the perfect way to use up snippets that have been discarded during conditioning. Bear in mind that you must get the flowers pressed as soon as you can after snipping, as you want them to look fresh and colourful.

Ingredients

· Blotting paper

· Large books

· Plastic bag

· Silica gel sachet

Recipe

1. Arrange your flowers, leaves and foliage on a sheet of blotting paper, making sure there is space between them and that there isn't any overlapping.

2. Place another sheet of blotting paper on top.

3. Find a large, heavy book that is bigger than your blotting paper (I find the *Oxford English Dictionary* or a big old encyclopedia just the thing!).

4. Open the book towards the back and carefully place your blotting paper and flowers inside. Close the book.

5. Place the book in a plastic bag with a sachet of silica gel, which will help with the drying process.

6. Stack more books on top and leave the pile somewhere cool and dry for about a week.

Blooms for Houseguests

If you've got someone really special coming to stay for the weekend, be it your best friend, your Godmother or your brother or sister, why not spoil them with some little floral flourishes?

A posy on the bedside table is essential (see Dinky Posy in a Vase, p. 30), but you could go the extra mile and twist some flowers around the bedroom mirror, or, better yet, trail jasmine around the headboard to scent the room and send your guest off into a perfumed slumber.

As romantic and gorgeous as it looks, I would refrain from putting flowers on the pillow – you don't want to risk an allergic reaction! However, leaving a little present on the bed is always a treat, and will make your guest feel like a VIP.

Recipe

I like to wrap a single boxed chocolate in pretty marbled paper, tie it with velvet ribbon and insert a few sprigs of blooms into the bow. The wrapping may cost more than the chocolate, but hey-ho! You will be the dream host and it will set the tone for a wonderful weekend together.

Bowl of Blooms

There is something very decadent about turning up to a dinner party with a bowl full of blooms. The bowl can be any shape or size, just make sure it's watertight. I remember when I was little a friend of my mum's turning up for a 'grown-up' dinner party with an ornate silver bowl filled with floating waterlilies – it looked magical!

I like to make this sort of arrangement very flower-heavy and keep it low to the bowl, as it looks fuller and more luxurious this way. It also means that your host can put it on the table as a glorious centrepiece that won't disrupt the flow of conversation.

Here, I keep the stems on the flowers for a more structured arrangement, but you could simply fill the bowl with water and float flower heads in it; the only thing you might struggle with is transporting it without spilling all the water. If you do want to float flower heads, carnations, roses and *Ranunculus* work well.

Ingredients

· Florist frog (optional, see tip)

· Florist adhesive tack

· Decorative bowl

· Chicken wire

· Florist pot tape

Foliage & flowers

I wanted to make this arrangement really luxurious and flower-heavy, so I used a ratio of one-quarter foliage to three-quarters flower.

· Foliage – Berried ivy, Camellia, pistache

· Flowers – Anemone, 'Carey' rose (David Austin), Double Frill anemone, Hellebore, 'Kate' rose (David Austin), *Ranunculus*, 'Sarah Bernhardt' peony, sweet-pea flowers and tendrils

♥ **Tip** — Florist frogs

It's not absolutely necessary to use a florist frog as well as the chicken wire; the chicken wire alone should provide sufficient support for the arrangement.

1. Stick some florist adhesive tack to the bottom of the florist frog and push it into the bottom of the bowl. Cut a piece of chicken wire and squash it into a loose ball inside the bowl.

2. Secure the chicken wire with a criss-cross of florist pot tape over the lip of the bowl. Fill the bowl about half-full with water.

3. Push foliage through the chicken wire into the water and on to the florist frog. The chicken wire should give you enough support to keep the basic structure in place. Don't be alarmed if the stems move: persevere and keep adding more.

4. Continue to add foliage until you have loosely covered the lip of the bowl – the leaves should look as though they're growing out of the bowl. Keep everything loose and natural.

5. The flowers should be kept quite tight at this stage, nestling within the foliage. Make sure you sit a big-headed flower in the centre to cover the florist frog, as this arrangement will be seen from above. Add the flowers in groups of two and three. The roundness of all the flowers used here means they complement one another and adds luxuriousness. I've also added some wayward stems; the anemone on the left and Double Frill anemones on the right seem to be tumbling out of the arrangement.

6. Now add more free-spirited flowers, varying the height and direction. Here the sweet peas and hellebores dance merrily out of the bowl.

Chapter IV

'In my mind, fashion and flowers are almost inextricably linked.'

An overview of my CV will show that it see-saws between two of my great loves: flowers and fashion. My first Saturday job as a young teenager was in the café at Painswick Rococo Gardens, the most exquisite example of baroque garden design that England has to offer. I served clotted-cream teas, slabs of treacle tart and effervescent elderflower pressé to botanical enthusiasts who would travel from all over the country (and beyond) in spring to see the snowdrops.

After leaving school I spent half my gap year as a stylist in a local branch of Topshop. It was hardly *haute couture*, but I loved being immersed in the collections and did my best to save as much money as possible to help fund my travels around India. But it was really while at the Courtauld Institute of Art in London studying for my degree in Art History that I realized I wanted to start my 'grown-up' working life in fashion, partly owing to the move of London Fashion Week and the circus of street-style photographers and fashionistas flocking like birds of paradise to my university campus, Somerset House on the Strand.

An opportunity for an internship came my way with the fashion designer Matthew Williamson, whose designs I had swooned over for years while poring over copies of *Vogue*, and a six-month placement somehow blossomed into nearly five years with the company. While there I was immersed in Matthew's wonderful world of print, embellishment and kaleidoscopic colour.

I was part of a tight-knit and fabulous team, and we travelled the world showcasing collections of his spirited, glamorous designs. I loved every moment but realized I had a calling back to nature: I really wanted to do something physically creative and work with my hands. So I took the leap and retrained as a florist. I set up my own company and the rest is history!

In my mind, fashion and flowers are almost inextricably linked. Both require an eye for colour, interesting palettes and unusual textural combinations. The principles of good design are intrinsic to both. It was a natural transition for me, and I believe my time working in fashion enhanced my attention to form and composition when working with flowers.

The practical combination of the two, the wearing of flowers as part of your 'look', is really just a bit of frivolity and fun. There is no way I can claim to waft around every day rocking flowers in my hair, since the reality of being a florist is that practicality is always at the forefront of my sartorial choices. So in winter I stick to machine-washable cashmere and jeans, preferably in inky shades of black and navy (you do get filthy doing this job) with robust rubber-soled boots and gloriously squashy puffa jackets. In summer it's all about cotton shirts, cropped trousers and loafers, so I can stay cool while zipping around doing floral errands. Not exactly glamorous, I know, but on the occasions when I can dress up I do love to indulge my one-time fashionista!

Corsage

I am championing corsages for the everyday –
no longer reserved for the mother of the bride!

I actually started to wear them a couple of years
ago, when having initial meetings about this book.
Previously I had turned up to meetings really
wanting to show how much I loved flowers, so I
would arrive with a little posy for the person I was
meeting, or *very* occasionally I would wear flowers
in my hair, but this started to feel unprofessional.
One day, dressed and ready to go in navy blazer,
white t-shirt and jeans (if in doubt, keep the
look classic), I had a few blooms left over from
an event, so I made a quick corsage and pinned
it to my lapel. It was the perfect thing to lift an
otherwise simple outfit, and looked fresh without
being pretentious.

It's now become a bit of a 'thing' that I do, and
I love pinning corsages to my blazer (it somehow
only really works on tailored jackets, perhaps
because they give the look a bit of formality and
then the flowers soften it down). Whether for
a business breakfast meeting or the pub on a
Saturday afternoon, ultimately this is just a bit of
floral fashion fun. They take moments to make, so
give it a go!

Ingredients

· Florist tape

· Ribbon

· Pins

Foliage & flowers

Remember that these flowers will be
out of water for the whole time you're
wearing them, so stick to robust stems
that won't wilt the moment you step out
of the front door.

· Foliage – Heather, Olive, Rosemary,
Soft *Ruscus*

· Flowers – Butterfly *Ranunculus*,
Lisianthus, Spray rose, Strawflower,
Waxflower

1. Start by gathering short pieces of foliage in your left hand, placing them next to each other with your right hand. Build this up until you have a little bunch of four or five sprigs. This will act as the backbone of your corsage. Add a few more sprigs of foliage, keeping it petite but varying the heights.

2. This is much like making a miniature version of the Floral Place Settings (page 58). You want to add flowers to the front of your little bunch, as the back will be kept flat against the outfit you pin it to.

Here I have used the taller *Lisianthus* and Butterfly *Ranunculus* at the back, and the bigger heads of the rose and strawflower at the front, with some waxflower buds to link them. Bind the stems together with a small piece of florist tape.

3. Cover the florist tape with a length of ribbon. I love using velvet in a contrasting colour – this wine-coloured one is just delicious!

4. Tie the ribbon in a knot, or a bow if you prefer (but I think the latter can look a bit twee). Trim the stems very short, so there is nothing to distract from your corsage. Secure to your outfit using a couple of pins.

Big, Blowsy & Bold Flower Crown

I couldn't disagree more with whose who declare that flower crowns are 'like, sooooo over'. I have made *hundreds* of these petalled pretties over the years – for garden parties, birthday queens, festival follies, masquerade balls and the odd fancy-dress outfit – proving their perpetual popularity. They make you look and feel like one of Titania's fairy followers.

I have always worshipped the Mexican artist Frida Kahlo, and in fact I dedicated a huge portion of my dissertation to her. Those striking images of her with hair braided, beribboned and topped with flowers are iconic, and definitely inspired me to create this recipe – the bigger the better, as far as I am concerned!

If you want to make something a little more understated, simply leave out the large-headed flowers (roses, *Ranunculus* and carnation) and increase the number of dainty flowers (waxflower, spray rose and rosebuds).

I would always suggest making this on the day it's required if you can, to give the blooms the best chance of surviving for as long as possible – nobody wants a wilty flower crown! If you have no choice but to make it the day before, submerge the crown in a big bowl of fresh water and store it somewhere cool overnight.

Alternatively, why not experiment with using all foliage for a green dream, or dried or fake flowers for something that will last longer than just one spin on the dance floor!

Ingredients

· Florist aluminium wire. If you can't get hold of this you can use garden wire, or tape together two lengths of sturdy stud wire

· Florist tape

Foliage & flowers

I would suggest going for a combination of big, open-faced flowers and some slightly smaller blooms so that you get a really full crown packed with an interesting variety of texture. Foliage is optional, but it's nice to have a little greenery to fill in any gaps that might appear as you build up this crown. Don't waste time conditioning the whole flower stem, since you will be cutting it down to about 10cm (4in).

· Foliage – Berried ivy, Rosemary, *Senecio*, Soft *Ruscus*

· Flowers – Carnation, Carnival *Ranunculus*, Cloni *Ranunculus*, *Lisianthus*, Rosebuds, 'Secret Garden' rose, Spray rose, 'Vuvuzela' rose, Waxflower

♥ Tip — Ribbon finish

If you don't have enough blooms, simply snip the wire where the flowers finish, make two loops in the ends of the wire and complete the circlet with beautiful ribbon at the back of your head.

1. Wrap the aluminium wire around your head to measure how much you need. Add an extra 10cm (4in) to each end and snip the wire. Place it on your work surface and plan where you want your flowers and foliage to go, so that you're sure you have enough blooms to go all the way round. I usually start with smaller blooms at either end of the wire and graduate towards the big babes at the centre, keeping everything facing one way.

2. The aim is to tape the stems directly to the wire. You can tape single stems or create small bundles of flowers and foliage, but avoid using more than two or three stems at a time, or the crown won't be stable.

3. Place the stem against the wire, using a length of florist tape to secure it. The process can be quite fiddly. Keep it fairly tight so that the stem stays in position. Wrap the whole stem, including the end, to keep in the moisture and give the flower the best chance of lasting the whole day.

4. Work down the wire, layering the next couple of stems over the previous one, covering the taped stems. Repeat this process until you have used up all your flowers and foliage.

5. Trim the stems as you work along the flower crown. This will stop the wire from becoming bulky and cumbersome.

6. Once the wire is fully covered, snip the florist tape off and finish the crown by hooking the extra lengths of wire together.

Botanical Makeup

I saw this during London Fashion week a few years ago, and fell head over heels. It transformed the models into living, breathing flower fairies, and I became obsessed with finding out how to re-create the look.

On the catwalk the makeup was a lot more extreme (imagine mouths that looked as though they were in full bloom, and faces covered in flowers like an overgrown garden), but if we take elements of that and just have little scatterings of tiny flowers it looks elegant and unusual. Think of it as like a temporary tattoo, only much more chic.

Once you have chosen your outfit, plan where you are going to arrange your florals. Here I'm wearing an amazing, drapey, off-the-shoulder dress, so I wanted to have a scattering of petals on my collarbone as well as around my eyes.

Ingredients

· Makeup wax or glue

· Tweezers

· Ready-pressed organic edible flowers (or press your own; see p. 100). I suggest using organic edible flowers, because they will be in direct contact with your skin. Think carefully about the colour palette, especially with regards to your skin tone and your outfit

· Makeup brush or fine paintbrush

Recipe

1. Dab a little makeup wax or glue in the spot where you want the bloom to stick.

2. Carefully use tweezers to put the blooms in position.

3. Press down the petals using a small makeup brush.

♥ **Tip** — Floral nails

To give yourself a manicure with a difference, why not use tiny flowers on your nails? Paint nails with one coat of clear or nude nail varnish. Allow to partially dry and, using tweezers, carefully place your flowers on the nail. Once the design is complete, seal with a layer of clear varnish.

Chapter V

Party

♥

'Having amazing florals at your party elevates and transforms your home.'

Nothing gets the party started like an incredible floral installation – it transforms your home from the ordinary to a place that is otherworldly! These creations are at the opposite end of the spectrum from where we started the book, which was focusing on creating easy, beautiful flowers for you to enjoy every day. Think of this chapter as the grand finale, reserved for those super-special moments in life that require a huge celebration – a big birthday party, a New Year's Eve bash or a surprise get-together thrown to announce an engagement.

Always consider flowers when planning your party, as they amp up the glamour and set the vibe for the evening. They show guests that you have thought about more than just the champagne and canapés, and will get people interacting. Flowers seem to have a magnetic pull; people want to be near them, look at them, touch them, smell them, so if nothing else they will be a conversation starter for guests and will definitely get people taking photographs and Instagramming! Having amazing florals at your party elevates and transforms your home, surprising guests and setting the tone for a fun and frivolous time. After all, flower displays like this are themselves rather frivolous, as most will only last for the night.

One of the most memorable parties I have worked on was for a client in Paris. It was at a beautiful apartment in the 7th arrondissement, a very chichi and prestigious part of the city, and there was no budgetary restriction or brief for the flowers, so I was able to let my imagination run riot. I wasn't able to visit the site beforehand, but the client sent me lots of photographs of the space and all the dimensions I could ask for. It was months in the planning and we eventually settled on an impressive design that included a full meadow walkway lining the entrance hall, an arch over the door, a mega mantelpiece installation and a hanging flower bonbon, plus bouquets for the 100 guests to take away with them as party favours. It goes without saying that I had my work cut out.

The apartment was even more beautiful and dreamy than the photographs had suggested, and with double-height ceilings and soft light, the interior was Parisian and perfect. But it was on the fifth floor of a grand old building, with a rickety one-person lift … quelle horreur! When the 200-plus big boxes of blooms arrived, there was only one way to get them into the apartment, and that was to carry them up the winding spiral staircase all the way to the fifth floor! I only had one tiny Parisian freelancer helping me, but somehow we became Herculean in strength and two hours later every stem was safely inside the apartment. It set us back in the schedule, but somehow we managed to work at lightning speed and the space was transformed into a *jardin des fleurs* just in time for dusk, when the guests arrived.

For your event you could do something similar to my Paris party and group a few recipes to create a stage set for your party, or you could focus on creating a single floral moment – all the recipes work just as well independently. My main advice when approaching this chapter is to have fun, be brave and give it a go!

Blooming Chandelier

I wouldn't advise swinging from this chandelier, but it sure is a fabulous way to get the party started. This is one of my favourite things to make, and is really popular at parties and weddings. I once made one that was 3.5m (11⅓ ft) wide and took three of us twelve hours to create yet only 20 minutes to dismantle. 'Tis the joy of floristry! I love that one of these adds another dimension to a space – it takes your eye *up* and transforms the room.

We are using floral foam in this recipe so that the flowers are able to drink, which means you can pretty much use any flowers you like. Choose a colour palette either to work with your party colour scheme (if there is one), or to look amazing in your interior.

Think about where you want to hang the chandelier, and make sure the area is structurally sound and able to take its weight. It is easiest to work in situ.

Ingredients

· Cable ties

· 4 sausages of floral foam, soaked the day before (see guidelines for preparing floral foam on p. 16). Dry them overnight so that when you're squeezing in the flowers, water won't come dribbling out

· Chair or stepladder – for working in situ

· Chain or fishing wire – to string up your chandelier. I like to use fishing wire because it's transparent, and makes the chandelier look as though it's floating, but here I have used chain because of the size and weight of the installation

· Hula hoop – try to get one in either black or green; it's easier to conceal

Foliage & flowers

· Foliage – Autumnal eucalyptus, English eucalyptus, Leatherleaf fern, Soft *Ruscus*, Viburnum

· Flowers – Anemone, Delphinium, Gloriosa lilies, *Lisianthus*, Phlox, *Ranunculus*, 'Raspberry Scoop' scabious, 'Secret Garden' rose

♥ **Tip** — foam-free

If you want to avoid using floral foam, use double the foliage to give a bushier base, and add florist test tubes containing single heads of flowers, securing them with additional cable ties or wire if necessary.

1. Having hung your hula hoop in position, use cable ties to attach the sausages of floral foam to the hoop at evenly spaced intervals. Cut four lengths of chain and secure to the hoop in the gaps between the foam. Hold the hoop up by the chain to check the weight is evenly distributed.

2. Start covering the hula hoop with foliage, tying it directly to the hoop with cable ties (it is best to reserve the floral foam for the flowers). Make sure you snip the cable tie excess as you work – you can see a couple of long ones in my picture. There is nothing more frustrating than hoisting something like this into position and then spotting a rogue cable tie!

3. Continue covering the hoop with foliage. The object is to cover it all the way round, so keep it wild and luscious – the bigger the better. Don't worry about the foliage not being in water. This is a one-hit wonder, and almost all types of foliage will easily last for as long as the party.

4. Now it's time to make this pretty and add your blooms. Consider the overall design of the chandelier when you're adding them, and distribute colours and blooms distributed all the way round.

Here I've used the hot-pink phlox and delphinium spires to get some colour and interest going around the chandelier. Push the flowers into the foam, as they will need water to last as long as you on the dance floor. Bear in mind that these pieces of foam are quite small, so take care not to push too hard or the stems will come shooting out the other side.

5. To complete the chandelier, add your babes. I wanted an explosion of colour, so I've contrasted bright red anemones with the hot pinks of the phlox and Gloriosa lilies.

Try to group these blooms together so the arrangement doesn't look too formal, and think about varying the height and direction of the flowers. You want to make it look as though the flowers are growing out of the chandelier, emerging from the sides and underneath as well as pointing upwards.

Flower Curtain

This is probably one of the floral installations I am most well known for. It all started with an installation at Topshop, and blossomed from there. Flower curtains create a petally perfect photo backdrop. Guests love getting a snap in front of them for Instagram, or they can be used in a doorway to mark the entrance to your soirée. Save this for a super-special celebration and wow your guests, all for minimal effort.

No matter how small your home is, there will be a spot where this could work – you just need to think creatively. It must be able to bear the weight of the installation, so plan carefully. If you're having your party in the garden and have a big tree, a flower curtain would look beautiful dangling from the branches.

I have two techniques for this sort of installation, one using ribbon and the other using coloured metallic reel wire. The steps show both together, but feel free to use one or the other.

Ingredients

· Pole. You need a support from which to hang your flower curtain. Here I am using a wooden broom handle, but you could also use a curtain pole or any other length of wood or metal

· Ribbons. Work out how much you need by measuring the space you are installing in and adding a little extra to allow for the tying. I tend to use a ribbon width of 2.5cm (1in)

· Metallic reel wire

· Paper-coated florist wire

Flowers

The flowers used in this installation will be out of water for the duration, so choose things that are going to last. They will also be hung upside down, so it seems a shame to waste a flower with an incredible centre, like an anemone, on this. Tall stems with lots of flowers, such as delphinium, foxglove and stocks, work particularly well aesthetically, as they follow the linear nature of the curtain. Before you begin, cut all the flowers down to an inch or so below the bloom. Too much stem adds unnecessary weight and can make it trickier to attach the flowers.

· Flowers – Carnation, Chrysanthemum, *Ranunculus*, Rose, Spider gerbera, Sweet william, Tulip

1. Using ribbon gives the installation a greater density and acts as a backdrop for the flowers. This is great if you plan to have people walking through the curtain, as the ribbon is silky and tactile and won't tangle as much as wire. Tie the ribbons to the pole, 3–5cm (1¼–2in) apart.

2. With wire, the process is a little quicker and there is a lighter, more magical quality to the installation because you don't see the mechanics. I think this technique works best installed in front of a wall so that you create a cool backdrop for photos.

3. When adding flowers to the wire, start at the top and work your way down, as it can get very tangled if you try to add one flower above another. Wrap the wire around the stem a couple of times. It should be tight enough that the stem doesn't slip out, but don't be too zealous, as you could snap it.

4. The benefit of using ribbon is that you can add flowers at any space on the length, in any order. Place the stem against the ribbon and wrap with a small piece of coated florist wire, twisting tightly to secure. I usually do this in quite an ad hoc way, in contrast to the methodical process for the wiring.

Meadow Box

When asked to describe my floristry style I always say it is 'meadow luxe', because I love all the wispy, dancing wild flowers you associate with a meadow and that give it movement and softness. But I also adore super-luxurious blooms that you wouldn't necessarily discover growing with the wild flowers – heavily perfumed, fully blown roses being a particular weakness.

These meadow boxes are one of my failsafe floristry party tricks. They are very versatile, and gorgeous when used as a centrepiece along a dinner table for a special supper, although take care not to make them too tall, as you don't want to obstruct conversation (unlike my example!). If you are lucky enough to have a fireplace, they look fabulous on a mantelpiece, or you can use them to line a stairwell or entrance hall.

Consider where the installation is going. If it is on the table or up the stairs, you will need flowers all around, but on the mantelpiece or against the wall you only need flowers at the front. If it's possible to arrange in situ, do so.

Ingredients

· Floral foam trays and blocks of floral foam, soaked beforehand (see guidelines for preparing floral foam on p. 16). Measure the space you are filling to work out how many you will need

· Florist pot tape

· Table knife

Foliage & flowers

· Foliage – Berried ivy, blossom, Guelder rose, Olive, Rosemary, *Senecio*, Soft *Ruscus*, *Spirea*

· Flowers – Butterfly *Ranunculus*, Carnival *Ranunculus*, Clematis, Cloni *Ranunculus*, Daffodil, Delphinium, grape hyacinth, Icelandic poppy, *Lisianthus*, *Oxypetalum*, *Ranunculus*, Snakeshead fritillary, Snapdragon, Strawflower, Waxflower

♥ Tip – Foam-free

Instead of using floral foam blocks and trays, use long, narrow vessels – small window boxes work, or ceramic planters or troughs. Make sure they are watertight, lining them with cellophane if necessary. Create a pillow of chicken wire slightly larger than the vessel and push it into place. Secure it with pot tape and fill the vessel with water.

♥ Tip – Moss

If you are struggling to cover your foam block completely, use moss to hide any unsightly mechanics once the meadow box is in situ.

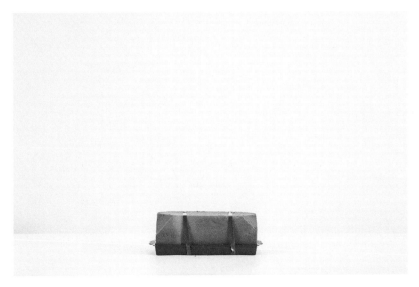

1. Place each soaked block of floral foam in its tray and secure with florist pot tape – I usually do this at two points on each block. Using a knife, slice off the corners of the foam (it's very satisfying, like going through butter, so you won't need a sharp knife).

2. Start by adding the foliage. These stems will inform the height of your design, so do keep this in mind. If you are making it for a table centre, I would suggest keeping the height below 30cm (1ft).

3. Keep building up the foliage until most of the foam has been covered. Because this is just one section of the meadow installation, I'm avoiding adding too much foliage at the sides, since the idea is that you build the blocks side by side in a linear manner.

4. Once you have covered most of the foam with foliage, begin to add the flowers. I always start with the tallest, as they encourage the meadowy feel and it's important to know what the height limit is. Here I have added a lovely bendy snapdragon on the left to draw the eye into the arrangement, and an even taller delphinium wafting above to take the eye up even further. The *Lisianthus* serve to fill in some of the spaces and add a delicious candyfloss pink.

5. Finally add the rest of the flowers. I've gone all out here and used a riot of different colours and varieties in what I would call a 'circus-style' palette, because it is so unashamedly colourful! Because I'm designing this for a table, I wanted to add something special that would be at my guests' eye level, so have included dainty snakeshead fritillary and grape hyacinth near the base.

Repeat with as many blocks as you like, and position side by side to form a seamless meadowscape.

Bloom Bonbon

One of the most fun things about being a florist is having the opportunity to dream up ways of installing flowers in interesting and unexpected places. This sprang from an idea to hang *something* above a pudding station at an event. It needed to be a floral installation that was as dense and luxurious as the dessert it hovered above! I had seen floral foam spheres at the market but never used one before, so I decided to experiment, adding the hanging baskets for stability, *et voila* – the bonbon was born!

I have kept this one fairly spherical, like a giant sweetie, as I find the symmetry very pleasing and it helps with the weighting of the installation. You could do something more asymmetrical, but if you do I would suggest hanging it in front of a wall (as opposed to in the middle of the room, as here) and focusing on flowering just the front of the bonbon.

I chose to use a lot of flowers because I wanted the arrangement to feel luxurious and indulgent, to tie in with the cocktail-party vibe, but you could easily make a bonbon using fewer flowers and more foliage. Just ensure you have a good selection of different types of foliage to give interest to the piece.

You can create miniature versions of this by using smaller floral foam spheres and wrapping them in chicken wire to secure. A series of little bonbons hung above a dinner-party table would look wonderful – I must remember to try this the next time I'm hosting a fun supper.

Ingredients

· Floral foam sphere

· 2 wire hanging-basket cages, large enough to hold the floral foam sphere, soaked (see guidelines for preparing floral foam on p. 16). Do this the day before to avoid drips

· Cable ties

· Carabiner clip

· Strong rope or chain

Foliage & flowers

· Foliage – Berried eucalyptus, Berried ivy, blossom, English eucalyptus, Heather, Leatherleaf fern, Olive, Pussy willow, Rosemary, Viburnum

· Flowers – Anemone, 'Blackberry Scoop' scabious, Carnation, Chrysanthemum, Clematis, Freesia, French tulip, Fringed tulip, Lilac, Peony, *Ranunculus*, Sea lavender, Sweet william, Waxflower

♥ Tip – Foam-free

Create a globe using moss and secure with chicken wire. Pop it inside the hanging-basket cage and work on the bonbon in the same way.

1. Place the floral foam sphere inside one of the hanging-basket cages. Put the other cage on top to form a globe, and fix together with cable ties. Hang your bonbon in position by attaching a carabiner to the top of the cage and either threading through strong rope or attaching a length of chain with cable ties. I would suggest attaching it to a strut or beam that can take the weight, as the whole installation does get quite heavy.

2. Insert some architectural branches and foliage to get the shape of your bonbon started. Cut stems at an angle and push directly into the floral foam. The hanging-basket cage will support the stems and keep everything in place.

3. Keep adding foliage until the sphere is covered. Think about where the bonbon will be viewed from. If it is hanging very high up, you will need to cover the bottom fully, but if it is closer to eye level you can get away with less coverage underneath.

4. Add filler flowers to pepper colour and texture throughout the design. Keep the stem length in line with the foliage – you want to create a full roundness rather than having flowers shooting out taller than the greenery.

5. Keep adding blooms until you have covered the bonbon. I wanted the colour palette to be opulent and rich, so I added dark 'Blackberry Scoop' scabious and burgundy *Ranunculus*, contrasting with hot pops of magenta and pink in the anemone and peony.

Archway

When I started out on my floral journey, the idea of creating an archway with a timber framework totally bewildered me. Then, one day I visited a family friend and there was a beautiful wrought-iron archway in the garden. It was overgrown with rambling roses and heavenly honeysuckle, but you could just see the structure beneath, and that's when I had my 'Aha!' archway moment! The answer to my worries stood before me: to use a ready-made garden arch as the framework.

Floral archways are really popular for events, perhaps because they give an immediate impression to guests even before they have entered the party. Then, as you walk through, it is as though you are being transported into a dreamy floral world! I personally don't think there is a better way to show your guests that they have arrived at your party. An archway also doubles as a gorgeous backdrop for photos of guests, framing them in flowers and foliage.

If space is limited around the doorway, you could stand the archway in front of a wall to create a pretty backdrop. Or, if you have a garden, an archway is a beautiful way to lead guests out from inside the house.

Ingredients

· Free-standing arch frame – find these at the garden centre or online

· 2 buckets filled with stones, pebbles, or anything that will add weight (optional)

· Floral foam garland and blocks in trays. The garland comes in a length of 12 pre-cut cylinders, which I snip into sections. All will need pre-soaking (see guidelines for preparing foam on p. 16)

· Cable ties

· Florist test tubes in varying sizes (optional)

· Moss (optional)

Foliage & flowers

Find some very large foliage branches for this installation, as these very quickly build up the form and coverage of the arch. They should be combined with shorter foliage to fill in any gaps, plus trailing pieces to wind around the arch and make it feel more natural.

· Foliage – Asparagus fern, Catkins, *Cocculus*, Foxtail fern, Laurel, Magnolia, Quince blossom, Soft *Ruscus*, *Spirea*, *Thlaspi*, Trailing ivy

· Flowers – Anemone, Butterfly *Ranunculus*, 'Combo' rose, Daffodil, Delphinium, 'Duchesse de Nemours' peony, *Genista*, 'Gloriosa' lily, 'Golden Mustard' rose, 'Harlequin' rose, Larkspur, Lilac, *Lisianthus*, Phlox, 'Raspberry Scoop' scabious, 'Rosalind' rose (David Austin), Sea lavender, 'Secret Garden' rose, Snapdragon, Waxflower, 'Yves Piaget' rose

1. Decide where your arch is going to be positioned and assemble the frame in situ. If necessary, stabilize it by placing the back two spokes in buckets filled with pebbles and stones (or anything that will add weight).

If you are assembling the archway outdoors you may be able to spear the framework directly into the ground. Position two floral foam blocks on either side of the base, angling the central ones in slightly.

2. Select large, leafy, heavy foliage branches. These will act as the foundation of your archway, and will help to cover the frame. Cable-tie them directly to the framework, using one tie at the base of the branch and a couple more further up the branch to prevent it from slipping.

Here I have used hardy foliage, so am not worried about them being without water, but if you are using foliage that is prone to drooping (such as hawthorn, whiteleaf or birch), stick the end of the branch into a large water-filled florist test tube.

3. Work evenly around the arch, ensuring that there is enough weight towards the back, for extra stability. Avoid attaching anything too heavy or bulky to the top of the frame. At this point you can begin to add foliage to the floral foam blocks at the base of the frame; select your tallest foliage for this, or anything that might wilt without water, and position it pointing upwards as though growing up and around the frame.

4. Secure trailing pieces of foliage at the top of the archway to unite the sides. I have used trailing ivy and feathery ferns for this, twisting them around the frame and securing with small cable ties where necessary. Keep this light, both from an aesthetic and a practical point of view, since anything heavy could compromise the archway's stability.

5. Keep building up the foliage until you have good, even coverage and have hidden most of the frame. The foliage should look bushy and natural. Here I have kept it fairly uniform in terms of distribution, but have avoided it looking too symmetrical by adding a stunning branch of magnolia buds on the left-hand side, and by using lots of different types of foliage and not worrying when it looked a little wild.

6. Step back from the archway and think strategically about where you want to position the flowers. I would always focus on the front that guests will approach first. Cut up the floral foam garland and attach individual pieces to the framework where you want the flowers to be.

Try to conceal them in the foliage. Don't space them too evenly or symmetrically – here I added one in the top left-hand corner of the arch, and another midway down the right-hand side.

7. I always keep the florals in the upper parts of the archway quite clustered, and focus on using the round-headed babes there. Here the roses, peonies and *Ranunculus* are working to their maximum petal-power! I like to group the flowers together, angling the stems upwards and outwards to mimic the way they might grow in nature.

Cut the stems at a sharp angle and push them firmly into the foam, taking care that they don't come out at the other side, as this will mean the flower cannot take on moisture. Work methodically, thinking about colour and type of flower. It is very easy to become too focused on one small area, so make sure you keep stepping back to check you are happy with the overall design.

If there are any areas of floral foam that haven't been covered with blooms, use small pieces of foliage or moss to conceal them.

8. To complete the arch, add flowers to the floral foam blocks at the base. I always reserve the tallest spires for this task, and here I have used pretty mauve delphinium and larkspur to add height and drama, connecting the base with the flowers higher up the archway.

When all the tallest flowers are in, work in some shorter ones in clusters around the base, emulating a garden border and adding intrigue and colour to the design. As before, cover any visible floral foam with small pieces of foliage or moss.

Blossomany

♥

Practical Stuff

Where to find flowers

My best advice would be to find a reliable local flower stand or florist that has a good selection of seasonal flowers and foliages. Buddy up with them and they should be able to order in special stems and bits that you are after.

Supermarkets also have an increasingly impressive offering available. One year I was able to get beautiful British-grown peonies at the supermarket cheaper than I could find elsewhere. Avoid buying the pre-made bouquets and instead go for single-variety bunches, as you would at the flower market, and style them in your own arrangements. If you can supplement with a little interesting foliage from the garden, or from the florist, then even better!

As I live in the UK, all my recommendations on this page are British-focused. For wholesale flowers in London, New Covent Garden Market (newcoventgarden market.com/flowers) is the biggest and best, open every day except Sunday. Go early and take cash. Colombia Road Market in east London (columbiaroad.info) is open only on Sundays. Other online florists include Bloom & Wild (bloomandwild.com) and The Real Flower Company (realflowers.co.uk).

Online you can find companies offering wholesale flowers to the public. Two I know in the UK are Triangle Nursery (trianglenursery. co.uk) and Dutch Flower Auction (dutchflowerauctiondirect.com). The benefit is that you get wholesale pricing, but as with New Covent Garden flower market, you must buy everything in wholesale quantities, so you wouldn't be able to buy 1 or 2 stems, but wraps of anything from 10 to 100 stems.

I am hugely passionate about supporting local flower growers. In Britain, Flowers from the Farm (flowersfromthefarm.co.uk) is an amazing site that features over 500 'members', mostly small businesses including farmers, smallholders and gardeners, who grow British blooms that are available to buy. The Members Map is a really helpful tool that connects you with artisan flower growers in your area. Although the height of the flower-growing season is during the summer months, don't hesitate to get in touch with growers at other times of year; they will often have incredible and interesting foliage available to buy that will transform your 'imported' arrangements.

Where to find props and vessels

Why buy something new when you can get something that has a history embedded within it and its own story to tell? I adore antique markets and spend as many weekends as I can trawling them. In the UK you can find out where the nearest ones to you are on the great Antiques Atlas website (antiques-atlas.com/dbevents/). My favourites are Portobello Road Market (portobelloroad.co.uk/ the-market/), Sunbury Antiques Market (sunburyantiques.com) and Tetbury, Gloucestershire. The last is not techically a market but a small town in the Cotswolds. It's a hub of antique hunting and attracts people from all over the world.

For non-antique props, you can find some stars on the high street too; my favourites are Zara and H&M Home for gorgeous linens and coloured glassware.

Extra bits and pieces

For ribbons, head to V. V. Rouleaux (vvrouleaux.com), which stocks over 5,000 ribbons, trimmings and braids. I also love the luxe velvet ribbons from Berisford Ribbons (berisfords-ribbons.co.uk) and bulk-buy them in jewel tones for both bouquets and presents. If you want to wrap your bouquet in something truly special, Shepherds is a heavenly paper shop in Pimlico, London. You can buy online at store.bookbinding.co.uk. For beautiful edible flowers, try Maddocks Farm Organics (maddocksfarmorganics.co.uk/).

Seasonal Heroes

Spring

March, April, May

Spring has sprung, for me, the moment I clap eyes on the first cluster of blossom. Seeing the familiar puff of powder pink on a branch of a cherry tree fills my heart with glee, as I know that *finally* I can shake off the chilly shackles of winter. Almost overnight everything seems to turn from dank to verdant: green shoots flare into full leaf and everywhere you look new life is popping up. Crocuses appear from nowhere, their regal, toadstool-like forms proudly standing among the green. The sky is filled with flocks of birds merrily chirping their return from warmer climes. Back home in the Cotswolds, the signs of new life are rife throughout the countryside: newborn lambs taking their wobbly first steps, baby bunnies and tiny chicks peeping into the spring sunshine. Everything feels joyful and full of hope as we march past the vernal equinox and on to longer days, yee-haw!

The flowers of spring vary from delicate bulbs that I like to think of as fairy dwellers – snowdrops, bluebells and lily of the valley could all provide perfectly proportioned habitats for a Tinkerbell-sized tenant – to some serious showstopper babes. I'm talking, of course, about the peony – one of the most (if not *the* most) loved and most 'favourited' flower I've ever known. Majestic in every way, the bloom is a bit of a bolshie show-off, but underpinned by its intricate arrangement of petals. The colours range from angel-cheek palest blush to buckeye burgundy, and the perfume is celestial. You cannot do anything but bow down to the peony, and I'm yet to come across anyone who disagrees.

Because spring brings such a variety of flowers, I find that my palette flips from super-sherbetty, such as lemon-meringue yellow, soft apricot and periwinkle blue, to poppy mauve and cherry-bomb pink. I think this is reflective of the fizz of excitement that spring brings: you can't resist being excited by colour, so don't be afraid to make mistakes!

My favourite spring flowers

· Blossom

· Bluebell

· Daffodil

· Fritillary

· Lilac

· Lily of the Valley

· Peony

· Ranunculus

· Solomon's seal

· Tulip

My favourite summer flowers

· Cosmos

· Delphinium

· Foxglove

· Japanese anemone

· Lupin

· Nigella

· Penstemon

· Poppy

· Rose

· Sweet pea

June, July, August

If I had to choose a favourite season, it would have to be summer. There's such vibrancy and vitality to this time of year, and everything you see and smell seems to be imbued with the glorious warmth of the sun high in the sky. Not to mention that I am a June baby, so it's when I get to celebrate my birthday! But honestly, there's nothing like summer in the city. Gardens brim with beauties ripe for the picking, in a rainbow fresco unlike any other, and the parks offer every colour you can imagine in their incredible borders, with butterflies and bumblebees merrily flitting from one to another. The heady air shimmers with the perfume of wild honeysuckle, freshly mown grass and something faintly like vanilla ice cream and strawberries.

As for the blooms, they are at their very best at this time of year. We become spoiled for choice, and I can use 100 per cent British-grown flowers at this time. Like a child in a sweet shop, I will happily overindulge in swathes of sweet peas and their twisty tendrils and go into raptures over the perfume of garden roses. Don't even get me started on the wild flowers, the little fairy-house-like penstemon, dancing nigella and bewitching foxglove. There is such an array of colour on offer during this time that you can be really creative and wild when it comes to choosing a palette. I tend to veer towards hothouse pinks and mauves, as I love the way they meld into a delicious summer-pudding colour scheme.

Autumn

September, October, November

The turn of the season from summer to autumn is
the most glorious thing to witness. The trees seem to
caramelize into a melee of toffee browns, burnished
ochres and molten-butter yellows. It all looks delectable.
There is a sense of fecundity, thanks to the abundance of
fruit and the miraculous second flush of roses, but also
one of wistfulness and the hope that we might get an
Indian summer. We cling on to the golden late sunshine,
but the tart coolness in the air that causes you to pull a
jumper around your shoulders signals that winter is just
around the corner.

This is a time for enjoying the here and now, and there
is no flower more apt for this than the dahlia. This
most exquisite flower, which can produce divine little
pom-pom heads the size of a ping-pong ball, can also
create beautiful beasts with heads the size of dinner
plates. For me autumn is all about the dahlia, a flower
that has been much maligned for many years as being
unfashionable and ridiculous. Thankfully now this
snobbishness seems to have dissipated and there is
definitely a dahlia uprising!

To reflect the turn in the season, my colour palette
always tends toward richness, an intoxicating mix of
rusts and bronzes spun with deep raspberry-reds and
the palest creamy pinks. Some of my favourite flowers
to use at this time sound like an order in a Parisian
boulevard café: 'Café Latte' rose, 'Café au Lait' dahlia
and 'Crème Brûlée' phlox – as delicious-sounding as
they are to look at.

My favourite autumn flowers

· Achillea

· Calendula

· Crocosmia

· Dahlia

· Echinacea

· Hydrangea

· Rose hips

· Scabious

· Verbena

· Zinnia

My favourite winter flowers

- Amaryllis
- Anemone
- Crab apple
- Cyclamen
- Daffodil
- Hellebore
- Hyacinth
- Juniper
- Magnolia
- Snowdrop

Winter

December, January, February

I know it's winter when I leave for the flower market in the early hours of the morning and there is a deep, dark sky studded with luminous stars. The night sky in winter is just so much more vivid than at any other time of year. There is a glassy opaline quality to the air, a frosted sparkling that dusts trees and fallen leaves. Winter sees the end of one year and the beginning of the next, and despite everything looking fairly greige, there is a palpable excitement in the lead-up to Christmas (and it goes without saying that I love this holiday). I also look forward to the new year, with hopes, wishes and dreams for the year ahead hanging in the air.

In preparing for Christmas I am quite the traditionalist and worship foliage – Scots pine, blue spruce, olive leaves, mistletoe kisses and any type of fir I can get my hands on. The scent of pine is strongly evocative of the festive season, and I like to enhance it with fruits and spices – exotic jewel-like pomegranate, dried mandarin and lime slices, crushed cardamom and cinnamon.

The new year sees the furtive beginnings of the British flower season, starting with the heroic hellebore, which can push through even the frostiest ground, and then the intensely scented daffodil and equally odoriferous hyacinth, which I adore for their tiny bell-shaped flowers. (Although I didn't love them so much when I had to make a bridal flower crown entirely from their tiny pips – I nearly went blind!) I like to keep my palette muted during this part of the season, as it seems appropriate after the indulgence of Christmas to keep it pared back.

Index

Page numbers in *italics* refer to the
    illustrations

Achillea 168
amaryllis 18, 169
anemone 18, 104–7, 128–33, *133*, 144–49,
    149, 150–59, 169
    double-frill 104–7, *107*
    Italian 34–35
    Japanese 167
arches and archways 126, 150–59, *151*,
    156, *157*, *158*, *159*
asparagus fern (for foliage) 46–49, 62–65,
    68–73, 74–79, *78*, 150–59, *157*
    foxtail fern 46–49
astrantia 21, 26–29, 92–95, *94*

beech (for foliage) 21, 40–45, *44*,
    80–83, *82*
birch (for foliage) 21, *156*
blossom 10, 50, 80–83, 92–95, 138–43,
    144–49, 166 *see also Prunus* blossom;
    quince blossom
blossoming teas 62
bluebell 166
bonbons of flowers 16, 126, 144–49, *145*,
    146–47, *148*, *149*
books 11, 100, 163
bottles *17*, 26–29, *27*, *28*, *29*, 58, *61*
bouquets 12, 86–87, *87*, 88, *90–91*,
    92–95, *93*, *95*
bud vases 12, *17*, 26–29, *27*, *28*, *29*

cake stands *62*, 62–65, *63*, *64*, *65*
Calendula 168
camellia (for foliage) 92–95, 104–7
candlesticks *16*, 46–49, *47*, *48*, *49*
carnation 46–49, 116–19, 134–37, 144–49
catkins (for foliage) 150–59
centrepieces 26, 74–79, *75*, *76–77*, *79*,
    104–7, *105*, *107*, 138–43, *139*,
    140–41, *143*
chain 15, 128, *132*, 144, *148*
chandeliers 128–33, *129*, *133*
chicken wire 12, 15, 16, *64*, *78*, *82*, 104,
    106, 138, 144
Christmas 50, 68, 269
chrysanthemum 50–53, 134–37, 144–49
clematis 66, 80–83, 88, 138–43, 144–49
Cocculus (for foliage) 40–45, 150–59
colour and colour schemes 10, 12, 34, 38,
    45, 50, *83*, 88, *94*, 110, *115*, 120, 128,
    133, *143*, *149*, 166, 167, 168, 269
compote arrangements 74–79, *75*,
    76–77, *79*
conditioning 12, 18–21, *19*, 58, *61*, *73*, 92,
    100, 116
corsages 12, 15, 112–15, *113*, *115*

cosmos 166
    chocolate 88
cotoneaster (for foliage) 80–83
crab apple 169
crocosmia 168
crocus 166
crowns 116–19, *117*, *119*
cyclamen 169

daffodil 21, 26–29, 74–79, 88, 138–43,
    150–59, 166, 169
dahlia 168
    'Café au Lait' 168
Daucus 40–45, *45*, 74–79, *79*, 80–83, *83*
delphinium 21, 40–45, *45*, 80–83,
    83, 128–33, *133*, 134, 138–43, *143*,
    150–59, 167
dried flowers 38–39, *39*, 50, 58, 116

echinacea 168
entertaining 56–57, 58, 62, 66, 74, 80
eucalyptus (for foliage)
    berried 50–53, 128–33, 144–49
    English 26–29, 40–45, *44*, 50–53,
        62–65, 88, 92–95, 128–33,
        144–49
euphorbia 18
everyday flower arrangements 24–25, 26,
    34, 38, 40, 50, 86
Exochorda ('magical springtime') 40–45,
    45, 80–83

fashion and flowers 10, 11, 24, 88, 110,
    120
fern, leatherleaf (for foliage) 46–49,
    62–65, *65*, 68–73, 128–33, 144–49
    see also asparagus fern
finding flowers 162
fir (for foliage) 50, 68, 169
floating flowerheads 104
floral foam 12, 15, 16, *16*, 46, *48*, 128, *132*,
    133, 138, *142*, 144, *148*, 150, *156*
florist adhesive tack 62, *64*, 104, *106*
flower curtains 134–37, *135*, *136*, *137*,
    170–71
forget-me-not 74–79
foxglove 18, 21, 124, 166
freesia 24, 50–53, 88, 144–49
fritillary 166
    snakeshead 138–43, *143*

garnishes 66, 66–67, *67*
Genista 26–29, 40–45, *45*, 50–53, *53*,
    92–95, *94*, 150–59
geranium (for foliage) 88
gerbera
    'Carbonara' 62–65, 80–83
    spider 134–37

gifts of flowers 86, 96, 100, 104
    see also bouquets
grape hyacinth 24, 138–43, *143*
grasses (dried, for foliage) 40–45, 58, 88
guelder rose (for foliage) 74–79, *78*,
    80–83, 138–43
gypsophila (for drying) 38

hanging installations 15, 16, 126, 128, *129*,
    130–31, *132*, *133*, 144, *145*, *146–47*,
    148, *149*
hawthorn (for foliage) *156*
heather 46–49
    for foliage 50–53, 58–61, 112–15,
        144–49
hebe (for foliage) 26–29, 92–95
hellebore 21, 26–29, 50, 96–99, 104–7,
    107, 169
holly (for foliage) 50
honeysuckle 88
    winter (for foliage) 40–45
hoops 128, *132*
hyacinth 88, 169
hydrangea 21, 168
    for drying 38–39, *39*

inspiration for arrangements 163
ivy (for foliage)
    berried 50, 68–73, 74–79, 92–95,
        104–7, 116–19, 138–43, 144–49
    trailing 50, 150–59, *157*

jam jars *17*, 26–29, *27*, *28*, *29*
jasmine 88, 102
    for foliage 68
juniper 169

larkspur 21, 40–45, 150–59
    for drying 38
laurel (for foliage) 150–59
lazy Susan 15, 74, 78
lilac 21, 30–33, *32*, 50–53, 88, 92–95, *94*,
    144–49, 150–59, 166
lily, 'Gloriosa' 128–33, *133*, 150–59
lily of the valley 66, 88, 166
Lisianthus 26–29, 30–33, *32*, 40–45, 80–
    83, *83*, 96–99, *98*, 112–15, *114*, 116–19,
    128–33, 138–43, *143*, 150–59
lupin 21, 167

magnolia (for foliage) 150–59, *158*, 169
makeup 120–23, *121*, *122–23*
mantelpiece decorations 15, 68, 74,
    126, 138
meadow boxes 138–43, *139*, *140–41*, *143*
meaning of flowers 86
mint (for foliage) 88
mock orange 88

Moluccella 40–45, *45*, 80–83, *83*
Monarda or bergamot (for foliage) 88
monkshood 18
moss (for wreaths, rings and arches) 50–53, *52*, *62*, 62–65, 138, 150, *159*
myrtle (for foliage) 88

Nigella 167
    for drying 38

oak (for foliage) 21
Oasis *see* floral foam
olive (for foliage) 26–29, 50–53, 112–15, 138–43, 144–49, 169
Oxypetalum 138–43

parties 126–27, 128, 134, 138, 144, 150
passion flower (for foliage) 68
penstemon 167
peony 21, 50, 56, 88, 144–49, *149*, 166
    'Doctor Alexander Fleming' 92–95, *95*
    'Duchesse de Nemours' 30–33, 150–59, *159*
    'Gardenia' 150–59, *159*
    'Sarah Bernhardt' 74–79, *79*, 80–83, *83*, 104–7
phlox 96–99, *98*, 128–33, *133*, 150–59
    'Crème Brulée' 168
pine (for foliage)
    pinecones 50, 68
    Scots 168
pistache (for foliage) 40–45, 104–7
Pittosporum, variegated and non-variegated (for foliage) 26–29, 96–99
place settings 58–61, *59*, *61*, *70–71*
poppy 21, 74–79, *79*, 167
    Icelandic 26–29, 138–43
posies *17*, *30*, 30–33, *31*, *32*, *33*, 58–61, *60*, *61*, 102, 112
potpourri 38
pressed flowers 100–101, *101*, 120–23, *121*
Prunus blossom 26–29, 50–53

quince blossom 40–45, 150–59

Ranunculus 21, 104–7, 128–33, 134–37, 138–43, 144–49, *149*, 166
    Butterfly 30–33, *33*, 74–79, 80–83, *83*, 92–95, *94*, 96–99, 112–15, *114*, 138–43, 150–59, *159*
    Carnival 46–49, 74–79, *79*, 116–19, 138–43
    Cloni 30–33, *33*, 46–49, 62–65, 74–79, *79*, 96–99, *98*, 116–19, 138–43
    Pon Pon 62–65
ribbon 12, 15, 58, *61*, 92, 96, 102, 112, *115*, 116, 134, *136*

rings for wreaths 50–53, *52 see also* hoops
rose 18, 21, 24, 88, 116–19, 134–37, 167, 168
    'Antique' 62–65
    'Bombastic' 80–83, *83*, 168
    'Café Latte' 74–79, *79*
    'Caramel Antike' 30–33, 92–95
    'Carey' (David Austin) 104–7
    'Combo' 150–59, *159*
    for drying 38
    'Golden Mustard' 62–65, 150–59, *159*
    'Harlequin' 150–59, *159*
    'Kate' (David Austin) 104–7
    'Keira' (David Austin) 80–83
    'Miranda' (David Austin) 26–29
    'Quicksand' 40–45, *45*, 62–65
    'Rosalind' (David Austin) 150–59, *159*
    'Secret Garden' 92–95, 116–19, 128–33, 150–59, *159*
    spray 80–83, *83*, 112–15, *114*, 116–19
    'Vuvuzela' 80–83, 116–19
    'Yves Piaget' 150–59, *159*
rose hips 168
rosemary 26–29
    for foliage 58–61, 88, 112–15, 116–19, 138–43, 144–49
Ruscus, soft (for foliage) 68–73, 74–79, 80–83, *82*, 112–15, 116–19, 128–33, 138–43, 150–59

safety issues 13, 18, 46, 62, *64*, 66
sage (for foliage) 88
scabious 80–83, 168
    'Blackberry Scoop' 144–49, *149*
    'Raspberry Scoop' 92–95, 128–33, 150–59
scent 24, 48, 88, 102, 126, 166, 167, 169
scissors 12, *13*, 18, *19*, 21
sea holly (for drying) 38
sea lavender 40–45, 80–83, *83*, 144–49, 150–59
seasonal flowers 10, 34, 166–69
Senecio (for foliage) 46–49, 58–61, 74–79, 80–83, 96–99, 116–19, 138–43
snapdragon 40–45, *45*, 80–83, 96–99, *99*, 138–43, *143*, 150–59
snowdrop 166, 169
Solomon's seal 166
Spirea (for foliage) 40–45, *44*, 80–83, 138–43, 150–59
spruce (for foliage) 169
statice (for drying) 38
stock 30–33, 88, 124
strawflower 112–15, *114*, 138–43
    for drying 38, 58
sweet pea 88, 167
    flowers and tendrils 24, 26–29, *29*,

30–33, *33*, 68, 92–95, *95*, 104–7, *107*, 167
sweet william 134–37, 144–49

table garlands 68–73, *69*, *70–71*
Thlaspi (for foliage) 40–45, *44*, 80–83, *82*, 150–59
toolkit 12–16
    conditioning 12–13, *13*, 18, *19*, 21
    cutting and snipping 12, *13*, 15, 18, *19*, 21, 46, *48*, *142*
    flower food 18, 21
    protection and care 12, 13, 18, *64*
    supporting and holding 12, 15, 16, 21, *64*, 74, *78*, *82*, 104, *106*, 128, 138, 144 *see also* floral foam
    tidying up 12, 15
    tying and binding 12, 15, *52*, 60, *61*, *64*, 68, *72*, *73*, 92, *95*, 114, *115*, 116, *118*, *119*, 134, *136*, *148*, *156*, *157*
    watering and spraying 15, 18, *53*, 68, *73*, 92, 128, *156*
tuberose 40–45, 80–83, *83*, 88
tulip 21, 134–37, 166
    French 144–49
    fringed 144–49

verbena 168
vessels 17, 138
    bowls 104–7, *105*, *106*, *107*
    compotes 74–79, *78*, *79*
    finding 26, 40, 162–63
    jugs 34–37, *35*, *36*, *37*
    pickle jars 12, 40–45, *41*, *42*, *43*, *44*, *45*
    urns 80–83, *81*, *82*, *83*
    vases 12, 30–33, *31*, 58, *61*, 96–99, *97* *see also* bud vases
    see also bottles; jam jars
viburnum (for foliage) 46–49, 68–73, 96–99, 128–33, 144–49 *see also* guelder rose
visitors, flowers for *102*, 102–3, *103*

waxflower 46–49, 80–83, *83*, 112–15, *114*, 116–19, 138–43, 144–49, 150–59
    for foliage 58–61
wearing flowers 110, *111*, 112, *113*, 116, *117*, 120, *121*, *122–23*
whiteleaf (for foliage) *156*
willow, pussy 144–49
wire and wire cutters 12, 15, *52*, *53*, 62, *72*, *73*, 116, *118*, 128, 134, *136 see also* chicken wire
wreaths 50–53, *51*, *52*, *53*

zinnia 168

Thanks

Writing this book has been a complete and utter joy and I couldn't have done it without the amazing support of so many people.

I had no idea what writing a book would entail, so embarked on this journey blissfully unaware of the immense amount of planning, hard work and thought that goes into it – and I could not have done any of this without the brilliant team at Laurence King. Without the wonderful commissioning editor Camilla Morton, this book would have remained a seedling of an idea, so thank you, Camilla, for believing in me and making the idea blossom into a reality. I'm so lucky to have you as a mentor and basically the blooming best blossomy cheerleader I know! Thank you also to my absolutely amazing editor Melissa Danny – your patience knows no bounds (and I know I have probably pushed you to the limit at times!). You have always offered me the kindness and reassurance I needed in times of stress.

Thank you to photographer James Stopforth for being so calm on set. I know the shoots were at times challenging – chasing the light during the shortest days of the year – but you have captured the flowers (and me) with such poise, and the results are just gorgeous. You are an incredible talent and I feel very lucky to have been able to work with you at the beginning of what will surely be a tremendous career.

To my amazing team, the 'Blossy Posse', I thank and salute you for all the brutal early starts, long days and bitterly cold conditions throughout the shoots. Would you believe we shot most of this in early January, and in fact the wreath was shot on the coldest day of the year? It was minus 3 degrees, but the sun was shining, and whilst I strutted around with in a little summer dress ignoring the goosebumps, my amazing team was on standby, shivering in the cold, ready and waiting with a hot cup of tea and a big puffa jacket to swaddle me in!). Huge love and thanks to Charlie Gozem, Camille Lambert and Jess Wheeler, my super-talented flower fairies.

Extra special thanks goes to dearest Harriet Slaughter, who helped me structure what was otherwise going to be a very rambling book! I can always count on you for a shoulder to lean on, sage advice and your exquisite taste and clever eye. Thank you also to Jay Archer, an awesome mentor and the first person to teach me to 'go big or go home!', which is most certainly where my love of maximalism began!

To the sweetest girls Frankie Daniella and my cousin Georgia Jansen, thank you for being such make-up mavens and working your magic on my poor sleep-deprived face. Not an easy task, I know! And thanks to Charlotte Tilbury's team for supplying such gorgeous make-up.

I have so many wonderful suppliers that I am lucky enough to work with. New Covent Garden Market is like a home away from home, and I thank everyone who works there, and my fellow florist troopers, for always making the ridiculous hours so fun. Special thanks to the teams at Bloomfield, GB Foliage, Pratleys and Zest for always sorting me out with the babes! Thank you also to the Daisyshop for the dried flowers, Nurtured in Norfolk for the edible flowers and Sandy at Devon Pressed Flowers who all came to my rescue at the last minute.

Thank you to the loveliest ladies Matilda Goad, Rose Lloyd Owen and Alice Levison. Matilda, your gold stripey jug is the dream, as are your bud vases – you're so clever! Rose, the cake was a total triumph, as were the petits fours and salads. Alice and the team at The Outnet, thank you for lending me such stylish looks and indulging the fashionista in me!

My darling Lucy Barlow – without you we wouldn't have had anywhere to shoot the book, so thank you for being so generous at such short notice and letting us invade the stunning home you share with your husband Josh and baby Figgy. You are an interior design genius, as I hope snippets of this book will show, and I have no doubt you are going to be an absolute superstar. I'm so lucky to count you as a dear friend.

Finally, thank you to my family. BB and Yo, you've believed in my floral dream since the beginning. You have never been anything but supportive – even when I called you in the middle of the night some years ago to announce I had had a moment of clarity (madness?) and was quitting my job to retrain as a florist. Thank you for always being available when I need you: on the phone when I'm having a meltdown, and for the countless hours you have spent traipsing up and down the country to help me on events when I was totally out of my depth. I love you both very much. Thank you for always encouraging me and the girls to follow our own paths. We are all incredibly lucky to have you both.

Carys and Bri – my sissys and besties. To know you are always by my side, no matter what, makes me feel like I can achieve anything. Thank you for always being there for me. I love you both more than you will ever know.

Last and by no means least, thank you to Johnny. The love of my life, my everything. Thank you for believing in me and for supporting me no matter what. Even if I've woken you up at 2.30am as I try (and fail) to creep around the house as quiet as a mouse ... or if I have commandeered your whole weekend to drive the van and act as lacky on an event. You are the best banker-by-day-florist-assistant-by-weekend I know – a true niche career! Your support never waivers, through the peaks and the troughs you are always there and always know the right thing to say, whether we are celebrating or whether I'm in dire need of having my spirits raised. I love your kind heart, generosity, calmness and fairness ... and most of all I adore your staunch belief that a lovely bottle of champagne is always a good idea! You are my world and I cannot wait to marry you.